THIS JOURNAL BELONGS TO

....

Jess MacCallum

THE
30-Day

Prayer
Challenge

JOURNAL
FOR MEN

BARBOUR
PUBLISHING

Published by Barbour Publishing, Inc., 1810 Barbour Drive, Uhrichsville, Ohio 44683, www.barbourbooks.com

Our mission is to inspire the world with the life-changing message of the Bible.

 Member of the
Evangelical Christian
Publishers Association

Printed in China.

INTRODUCTION

Welcome to *The 30-Day Prayer Challenge Journal for Men*!

After a daily reading that will help you see things the way God does, there are some questions to help you learn from your own thoughts and experiences about that topic. Do your best to be honest as you explore your answers, because that's the only way to really grow. Your responses to those questions will help you apply the truth to your life. Then, three prayer focuses—morning, afternoon, and evening—will keep you thinking and praying about that topic all day so it will take root in your heart.

The thirty days of focus will show you how important and beneficial it is to be in the Word of God daily and how much of an impact regular prayer times will have on your life. Pay attention to how your attitudes and expectations are changed as you spend time with Jesus and how you begin to look forward to that time each day. Plan now to take those practices forward beyond these thirty days and make them a part of the rest of your life.

DAY 1
BEING A MAN

As David's time to die drew near, he charged Solomon his son,
saying, "I am going the way of all the earth. Be strong, therefore,
and show yourself a man. Keep the charge of the LORD your God,
to walk in His ways, to keep His statutes, His commandments,
His ordinances, and His testimonies, according to what is
written in the Law of Moses, that you may succeed in
all that you do and wherever you turn."
1 KINGS 2:1–3 NASB

Solomon had the unique though difficult blessing of being at his father's
side as he was dying and to hear his father's last words. Few men get
that kind of farewell, and fewer still get the life-directing exhortation that
would guide Solomon as the next king of Israel. It's a moving encounter
and a turning point in the history of Israel.

David was an impressive man who lived a larger-than-life story.
As a teenager, he was a faithful shepherd who slew bears and lions
while defending his flock (1 Samuel 17:36). He was a gifted songwriter
and musician whose songs fill more than half the book of Psalms. He
rose from obscurity to become the most famous giant-slayer in history
(1 Samuel 17). As a man he led armies and won wars. He was a successful politician and became a popular and honored king, feared by the
nations that surrounded Israel (1 Chronicles 14:17). And though he had
his failings, he was remembered as one who led with integrity:

With upright heart he shepherded them and
guided them with his skillful hand. Psalm 78:72 ESV

No question about it, David was a "man's man" and about as successful
as a man can get. And Solomon had some pretty big boots to fill.

But as his life was drawing to an end, what did David point to as the
basis for being a man? His accomplishments? His heroism in battle?
His reputation? No. Did he tell Solomon that he had to do battle or
rescue the nation to be a man? No. David had a different perspective of
what it takes to be a man: keeping "the charge of the Lord"–following

wholeheartedly the ways God had revealed. And that, he well knew, would take more courage than facing bears, lions, giants, or armies. David clarified things for Solomon so all the other issues he would potentially wrestle with in life as a man—purpose, success, legacy, leadership—would fall into place. David did not want Solomon to be distracted by what the world says a man is but to be a man in God's eyes first and foremost. If there was a "secret" to David's success to pass along to his son, that was it.

Solomon's defining moment had come, and with it the weight of a kingdom, but also the blessing of being set on the right course. For all men, in all circumstances, being on the firm foundation of God's will makes a man succeed as a man.

▶ What was I raised to believe about manhood?

....
....
....
....

▶ Today, can I honestly say my idea of manhood is established on honoring God?

....
....
....
....

▶ Is there anything I can let go of that's keeping me from becoming God's kind of man?

....
....
....
....

▶ Whom do I influence as a man, and what kind of influence am I being right now?

....
....
....
....

MORNING:

**Thank God for your successes, and ask for help
against the world's definition of success.**

Something like this. . .

*Lord, I thank You for all that You have done for me. I pray
that throughout each day, You will aid me in the constant
battle against the temptations of greed, lust, and power,
which the world uses as the definitions of success. Lord,
please help me remember that any success I have comes
from You. I pray that in all things I would honor You.*

AFTERNOON:

Ask God to craft you into His kind of man.

Something like this. . .

Lord God, I pray that You will help me understand what it truly means to be a man of God. I pray that You will help me walk in Your ways in all that I do and keep Your charges wholeheartedly. I ask that You change me from what the world says I should be, into the kind of man You want me to be, so that I may always serve You to the fullest.

EVENING:

Confess the things stopping you from being the man
God has called you to be, and ask for help being
a good influence on those around you.

Something like this. . .

*Father, I confess and ask forgiveness for all the things I
have let keep me from being the man You made me to be.
Change me and help me succeed as a man who stands
strong on the foundation of Your will, that I might be
an example of Your mercy and love at work.*

....
....
....
....
....
....
....
....
....
....
....
....

DAY 2
OUR TRUE BATTLE

What is causing the quarrels and fights among you?
Don't they come from the evil desires at war within you?
JAMES 4:1 NLT

The inner life of a man is the real life of a man. What we think about, what we dwell on, is who we truly are, or will become. Proverbs 23:7 (NASB) puts it this way: "For as he thinks within himself, so he is." The heart—or inner life—will determine everything that we do and say over time since from it comes an internal value system. That's why we are warned:

*Guard your heart above all else, for it determines
the course of your life. Proverbs 4:23 NLT*

One of the clear warnings of scripture is that the inner life of a man will always come out; it will always manifest itself in some way. Jesus made it clear that what we store away in our hearts will show up in our daily lives, for better or for worse:

*"The good person out of the good treasure of his
heart produces good, and the evil person out of his
evil treasure produces evil, for out of the abundance
of the heart his mouth speaks." Luke 6:45 ESV*

So, when we experience conflict with others—spouse, kids, coworkers, neighbors, other believers—we may be allowing the inner turmoil of our own heart to manifest itself in those relationships. We may have stored up the wrong things inside and allowed them to cloud our judgment. We may be engaging in the wrong battle! Other people may not be "the problem." And if we engage in the wrong battle, we'll be wasting our energy and growing more frustrated at the same time.

The real battle is against "worldly desires that wage war against your very souls" (1 Peter 2:11 NLT). Buying into worldly passions will fill us with agitation and unrest. Our efforts should focus on submitting our hearts to Christ and allowing Him to pour into us His love and peace, filling us with His "good treasure":

*"I am leaving you with a gift—peace of mind and heart.
And the peace I give is a gift the world cannot give.
So don't be troubled or afraid." John 14:27 NLT*

There is nothing this world can offer like the peace of Christ. A heart consumed with His peace is a heart that doesn't easily lose its temper, that won't respond to people harshly or retaliate in kind. Rather than insist on its own way, the peace-filled heart values unity with others:

*With all humility and gentleness, with patience, showing tolerance
for one another in love, being diligent to preserve the unity of
the Spirit in the bond of peace. Ephesians 4:2-4 NASB*

The good news for us is Christ has overcome the world, conquered death, fulfilled the Law, and crucified the flesh—all of which He shares with us in our salvation. He reconciles us to God, to ourselves, and to others. Now we can be free to fight the good fight of faith and face our proper enemy:

*For our struggle is not against flesh and blood, but against
the rulers, against the powers, against the world forces of this
darkness, against the spiritual forces of wickedness
in the heavenly places. Ephesians 6:12 NASB*

▶ Am I experiencing any kind of conflict with others? At work? At home? At church?

....
....
....
....

▶ Have I resisted humbling myself even when I knew it could resolve or improve a strained relationship?

....
....
....
....

▶ Does the peace of Christ characterize my inner life? How am I storing up "good treasures" in my heart?

....
....
....
....

▶ What can I begin doing (or do more of) to fight the real enemy more effectively?

....
....
....
....

MORNING:

**Pray that God would help you guard
your heart throughout the day.**

Something like this. . .

*God, please help me to steel my heart against the
things that are not of You. Please, Lord, be my shield
in the struggle against selfish desires, and instead,
help me focus on loving and serving those around
me with a heart that overflows with goodness.*

....

....

....

....

....

....

....

....

....

....

....

AFTERNOON:

Ask God to aid you in humbling yourself when resolving conflicts.

Something like this. . .

Heavenly Father, I pray that You will help me conquer my own pride and the selfish resistance I have toward humbling myself. Give me the strength and peace to resolve conflicts in a way that represents You, regardless of whether or not I am in the right.

....

....

....

....

....

....

....

....

....

....

....

....

EVENING:

**Ask Him to give you a heart of service and
to renew and refresh your mind.**

Something like this. . .

*Good Father, I have been fighting the wrong battles for
so long, and the overflow of my heart has caused conflict
with those I love and seek to serve. Please renew and refresh
my mind from the evil things I have dwelled on. Grant me
peace so that I may better focus on being an example
of Your love and sacrifice to those around me.*

DAY 2

DAY 3
WORSHIP

And David danced before the LORD with all his might,
wearing a priestly garment. So David and all the
people of Israel brought up the Ark of the LORD
with shouts of joy and the blowing of rams' horns.
2 SAMUEL 6:14-15 NLT

God designed men to be strong of course, but also to be caring and patient; to be confident, but also vulnerable and open to change. But many men find it more comfortable to exert their strength and hide their emotions—even before God and His people.

True masculinity is made complete in worship. Where else can a man open himself so completely without fear of failure, without pretending to be strong or competent or in control? Where else can a man be so honest without fear of being taken advantage of? Where else can a man stand rejoicing with no concern for judgment? Where else can a man look into the face of the most authentic Man of all?

To worship as a man means to ignore (or choose to ignore) what others think of your openness, the way King David did. Not long after David was crowned king, he led his army into battle to recapture Jerusalem. Once he established that city as his own, it was time to bring Israel's most prized possession back home—the ark of the covenant. It was a truly spiritual event for the entire kingdom. And David celebrated it openly and wholeheartedly! He cut loose in front of all his people in his raw enthusiasm for the Lord. But when his wife, Michal, (the daughter of the late king Saul whom God had removed from the throne in favor of David) saw it, she disdained David and rebuked him for this energetic public display. This was beneath the dignity of a king! David responded:

> "I was dancing before the LORD, who chose me above
> your father and all his family! He appointed me
> as the leader of Israel, the people of the LORD,
> so I celebrate before the LORD." 2 Samuel 6:21 NLT

Basically, David didn't give a rip what people thought of him when he was worshipping, even the members of his own household. David cared only for God's opinion. As a king, a warrior, and a shepherd he had faced death from man and beast, so public opinion wasn't about to scare him away from worshipping with all his might. In fact, David connected his position as the leader of "the people of the Lord" with the very reason he celebrated so openly.

Jesus said, "God is spirit, and those who worship Him must worship in spirit and truth" (John 4:24 NASB). Those are two things that should not be contained by fears of embarrassment or public opinion. This is not to suggest all worship is to be as exuberant as David's was on the occasion of the return of the ark, but when the Spirit moves us to express joy, we must be careful not to quench His exuberance within us.

So, as the Holy Spirit leads, express yourself in worship—confessing, singing, crying, even dancing with wild abandon before your Maker, your Redeemer, your Lord—not concerning yourself with those who might look on, with those who might be quick to find fault. You'll be expressing your masculinity, not relinquishing it. It will be leadership by example to all the people.

....
....
....
....
....
....
....
....
....

▶ Is there anything about other people's opinions that is holding me back from worshipping the Lord openly?

....

....

....

....

....

....

▶ What would I do differently in worship or prayer if I were alone?

....

....

....

....

....

....

▶ Can I help others worship by being less concerned about how I appear when I come before God to worship?

....

....

....

....

....

....

MORNING

Ask God to help remind you throughout the day that your worth doesn't come from what others might think.

Something like this. . .

Lord God, as I go about my day today, remind me that my worth comes only from You. Please help me to see past people's opinions and what the world deems as masculine, and instead be open in my love and praise of You.

....

....

....

....

....

....

....

....

....

....

....

....

....

AFTERNOON

Ask God to help you be someone who can lead by example with "abandon."

Something like this. . .

Faithful Father, I ask that You free me from the confinement of ego and fear of judgment. Worshipping and praising You is not beneath anyone's dignity, Lord! Help me become one who leads by example and loves You with abandon.

....

....

....

....

....

....

....

....

....

....

....

....

EVENING

Ask God to give you the courage to be vulnerable.

Something like this. . .

*Lord, help me to find the courage to be vulnerable and
open in my everyday praise and worship of You. Help me
to stand firm and to see that the world's idea of being
"manly" is just a prison, because true strength and freedom
come from being unafraid to rejoice in You.*

DAY 4
WISDOM

For wherever there is jealousy and selfish ambition, there you
will find disorder and evil of every kind. But the wisdom from
above is first of all pure. It is also peace loving, gentle at all times,
and willing to yield to others. It is full of mercy and the fruit
of good deeds. It shows no favoritism and is always sincere.
And those who are peacemakers will plant seeds of
peace and reap a harvest of righteousness.

JAMES 3:16–18 NLT

It's no surprise that men are competitive. From professional sports leagues (which are predominantly male) to a "friendly" game of golf among buddies, the natural compulsion to win comes out. In the right context, competition can be exhilarating; it can build the bonds of new friendships and reinforce old ones. But taken to extremes competition can be destructive, even devastating.

History is filled with the bitter and ruinous rivalries of political, military, and business leaders. Countless millions have been caught up in the vain competition for power and control of a few. Countries have gone to war over the personal ambitions of a single man. In fact, James may have been thinking of current events when he wrote today's verse—the Roman Empire was built on the blind ambition of its leaders, although Roman historians often painted a glorious picture of Roman conquests. Even today, some leaders point to the "wisdom" of the ruthless, Machiavellian men they admire. "It worked for them!" is the justification.

But James makes a clear and necessary distinction between worldly and heavenly wisdom. Man's wisdom is common; God's wisdom is uncommon. Heavenly wisdom never destroys or deceives but builds and unifies. The "wisdom from above" strives for purity and peace, goodness, and a concern for others. It's unselfish in every way and is not judged by the "results" alone. The wisdom of God is the source of true riches and true contentment. As King Solomon declared:

How blessed is the man who finds wisdom and the man who
gains understanding. For her profit is better than the profit of

silver and her gain better than fine gold. She is more precious than jewels; and nothing you desire compares with her. Long life is in her right hand; in her left hand are riches and honor. Her ways are pleasant ways and all her paths are peace. She is a tree of life to those who take hold of her, and happy are all who hold her fast. Proverbs 3:13–18 NASB

And best of all, heavenly wisdom is free for the asking:

If you need wisdom, ask our generous God, and he will give it to you. He will not rebuke you for asking. James 1:5 NLT

Not promoting ourselves or not pushing past others may seem naive in today's dog-eat-dog world. Giving up our rights in order to seek peace with someone may look foolish. Not retaliating even when justified may not appear wise to those urging us to stand up for ourselves. Refusing to engage in conflict to move ahead may label us weak or fearful, unable to rise to the challenge. But God's wisdom transcends the "wisdom" of self-promotion and the hollow trophies of this world. As the martyred missionary Jim Elliot once observed, "He is no fool who gives what he cannot keep to gain what he cannot lose."

▶ Is there any area of my work life that I need to reevaluate using the criteria that James calls "the wisdom from above"?

....

....

....

....

....

....

▶ Do I have any unhealthy rivalries that I can confess and abandon?

....

....

....

....

....

....

▶ How can I pursue my goals in life using God's wisdom and not the world's? What would that look like?

....

....

....

....

....

....

MORNING

Ask God to help you reevaluate the decisions you make with His wisdom.

Something like this. . .

Wise Father, aid me with Your wisdom in my day-to-day decisions and relationships. Please help me to replace my jealousy, spite, and selfish ambition with mercy, love, and the strength of patient wisdom.

AFTERNOON

Ask God in humbleness to help you confess and
overcome areas in your life where you aren't being wise.

Something like this. . .

*God Almighty, I confess that I struggle with making unwise
and unhealthy decisions, to my own harm. I pray that You
will give me the courage to tear down the idols I've built
and grant me the strength to overcome the temptations
of the world's "wisdom." Instead, help me constantly
look to Your eternal wisdom for guidance.*

....

....

....

....

....

....

....

....

....

....

....

....

EVENING

**Ask God to help You pursue Your goals
with wisdom and a healthy, uplifting spirit.**

Something like this. . .

*Father, when pursuing my goals in life, help me do so with
a loving and wise perspective. I pray that any competitions
I have will be healthy and build bonds. I want to be careful
to not justify unwise decisions in the name of results.
I reject the world's wisdom and pray for Your
wisdom to guide me in all that I do.*

....

....

....

....

....

....

....

....

....

....

....

....

DAY 5
SUCCESS

If the iron is blunt, and one does not sharpen the edge,
he must use more strength, but wisdom helps one to succeed.
ECCLESIASTES 10:10 ESV

Men are naturally drawn to success—seriously, who sets out to fail? Consequently, most of us love a challenge. . .as long as there's some possibility of winning. In fact, if we're really honest (and just a little self-aware) we'd have to admit that we actually pull back from things in which we do not feel we can succeed; we inherently move away from anything that is likely to end in failure. That might be a good thing, if you're looking for the right job or career path. If you want to be a jockey but weigh north of 120 pounds, you're not likely to see much success in that field. In that case, quitting might be exercising wisdom.

But sometimes the arenas we mentally or emotionally "quit" include those of the greatest value. Marriage, family, friendships, church. God Himself perhaps. If we don't see a path to succeed, if we consider these areas too much work for too little return, we might be tempted to pull back. We might not even notice we've redirected our efforts to areas we enjoy more. We could be abandoning the more important things for the easier things, sometimes with devastating consequences. But it doesn't have to be that way.

If you've ever tried to cut down a tree with an ax instead of a chainsaw, you know how much work it can be. And if you've ever tried to do it with a dull ax, you know it's basically impossible. Common sense tells us that it's better to take the time to sharpen an ax beforehand, otherwise you'll just wear yourself out. If you're constantly frustrated in some area of your life, maybe you're banging away with a dull ax; maybe you simply lack wisdom in that area and need to gain the right understanding.

The challenge of this proverb is to identify where we are exhausting ourselves and to take the time to seek God's wisdom that can lead us to success. Thankfully, He promises to give wisdom to those who ask:

*If you need wisdom, ask our generous God, and he will give it
to you. He will not rebuke you for asking. James 1:5 NLT*

*The Lord was pleased that Solomon
had asked for wisdom. 1 Kings 3:10 NLT*

Once you've asked for wisdom, seek it also. The book of Proverbs extols the blessings of gaining wisdom over and over:

*Blessed is the one who finds wisdom, and the
one who gets understanding. Proverbs 3:13 ESV*

*Getting wisdom is the wisest thing you can do!
And whatever else you do, develop good judgment.
If you prize wisdom, she will make you great. Embrace her, and
she will honor you. Proverbs 4:7-8 NLT*

Once you've asked for wisdom, and sought it, and found it—then apply it!

*Give me understanding and I will obey your instructions; I will
put them into practice with all my heart. Psalm 119:34 NLT*

Wisdom, like faith, is dead apart from action. The work we must do to be successful before God in the most valuable areas of life deserves the time and effort it takes to do it with His wisdom, in His way. Take time to get sharpened and set aside the time to stay sharp.

....

....

....

....

....

....

....

....

▶ Where am I experiencing frustration or failure on a regular basis? Is this something God has called me to, or am I free to choose another route?

....
....
....
....

▶ What does success look like in my personal life? What goals have I had for years with no real results? Losing weight? Getting on a budget? Sharing my faith?

....
....
....
....

▶ In my relationships, does sharpening the ax mean becoming a better listener? Being more patient? Controlling my temper?

....
....
....
....

▶ How do I plan to get wisdom on a regular basis?

....
....
....

MORNING

Pray that God would show you areas where
you need to step back and seek wisdom.

Something like this. . .

*Dear God, thank You for the opportunities You've given me.
Help me to pause and seek Your will in each one of them,
and give me fresh understanding for each.*

AFTERNOON

Ask God to give you a new perspective on serving
Him in those areas where you feel inadequate.

Something like this. . .

*Faithful Father, help me to serve You even when I don't
see results. Help me to see the value in the people and
situations You've brought into my life. Give me the
courage to face tough challenges without pulling back.*

....

....

....

....

....

....

....

....

....

....

....

....

....

EVENING

**Ask Him to give you a heart that seeks wisdom
and pursues it, and applies it at every opportunity.**

Something like this. . .

*Lord God, we both know I am inconsistent in what
I seek, often to the point of distraction. Give me a new
focus on seeking You and the wisdom You promise.
Show me what I need to let go of in order to please
You and walk more wholly in Your ways.*

DAY 6
GOD'S PROMISES

> And because of his glory and excellence, he has given
> us great and precious promises. These are the promises
> that enable you to share his divine nature and escape
> the world's corruption caused by human desires.
> 2 PETER 1:4 NLT

What's the point of salvation? Becoming a better person? Having a mission to give your life meaning? Getting into heaven when you die? Arguably those things might be enough from a human perspective, but God has something more in mind for us—something far more interesting and exciting.

God promised that when we joined His family we would become like our brother Jesus. Paul, like Peter, understood what God was offering His born-again children when he exhorted the believers in Corinth to act on the promises of God:

> *Therefore, having these promises, beloved, let us cleanse
> ourselves from all defilement of flesh and spirit, perfecting
> holiness in the fear of God. 2 Corinthians 7:1 NASB*

And what exactly are these promises from God that both Paul and Peter believed to be the motivation for this holy life? That God Himself would live among us, His people, and be our God; that we would be set apart from the world, even counted as His sons and daughters:

> *"I will make my dwelling among them and walk
> among them, and I will be their God, and they
> shall be my people. Therefore go out from their midst,
> and be separate from them, says the Lord, and touch
> no unclean thing; then I will welcome you, and I will be a father
> to you, and you shall be sons and daughters to me, says the
> Lord Almighty." 2 Corinthians 6:16-18 ESV*

God's plan, as incredible as it may sound, is that we should partake in, enjoy, and reflect His own divine nature. He wants sons (and daughters) who look and sound and act like Jesus—children that reflect His character and thinking; children who are, like His Son, free from corruption inside and out. God's plan from the beginning (long before we were born) was for us to share in His very image:

> *For those whom He foreknew, He also predestined to become conformed to the image of His Son, so that He would be the firstborn among many brethren. Romans 8:29 NASB*

God's offspring have one path to follow: living as freed and holy sons. Freedom and holiness are our inheritance, and we access it through the Holy Spirit:

> *And I will give them singleness of heart and put a new spirit within them. I will take away their stony, stubborn heart and give them a tender, responsive heart. Ezekiel 11:19 NLT*

> *And when you believed in Christ, he identified you as his own by giving you the Holy Spirit, whom he promised long ago. Ephesians 1:13 NLT*

The role of the Holy Spirit is to empower God's people to freely and honestly interact with the Father, taking hold of His promises daily. Without Him working in us—actually dwelling in us—nothing in our experience will ever truly change and the Father won't get the child He's after. Only when we rely on His presence in us to make us into the image of Christ will we take hold of the fullness of salvation promised in this life—and glorify our Father as sons who bear His name.

▶ Does God's promise to live in me and to change me into the likeness of Christ have a real impact on my daily life? Does it give me hope?

....

....

....

....

....

....

▶ Are there areas of my life that I've just "accepted" as they are, but conflict with being a good son to my heavenly Father?

....

....

....

....

....

....

▶ Am I excited about becoming like Jesus, or does it feel like a burden? What does that tell me about my understanding of my salvation?

....

....

....

....

....

....

MORNING

Ask the Lord to help you to be open each day to His changes.

Something like this. . .

Father, please open my heart each day to the changes You would make in my life. Lord, I want Your promises to be always at the forefront of my mind, so that I may better focus on what You have planned for me.

AFTERNOON

Confess to Him the areas in your life where
you remain unwilling to accept His changes.

Something like this. . .

*Lord Almighty, I confess that I have been stubborn in my
ways. In Your infinite mercy You protect me against
the apathy of just accepting things as they are, and that
through reflection on Your loving promises, I will
embrace each change with a renewed spirit.*

....
....
....
....
....
....
....
....
....
....
....
....

EVENING

Thank God for working in your life to change you, and pray for the courage to rely on Him throughout those changes.

Something like this. . .

*Thank You, Almighty Father, for working in my life
and shaping me into the man You desire me to be! You're
generous in Your plan for us, and I pray for the courage and
understanding to trust You during the most challenging of
trials and throughout the hardest of changes. Thank You!
You dwell within me, changing and molding me into
a son that bears Your glorious name!*

....

....

....

....

....

....

....

....

....

....

DAY 7
FAITH VS. FEAR

"My righteous one shall live by faith, and if he
shrinks back, my soul has no pleasure in him."
HEBREWS 10:38 ESV

People usually assume that doubt is the opposite of faith. But in the New Testament (NASB) the words *doubt* or *doubting* appear only a handful of times, while *fear* or *afraid* show up over one hundred times. While we can't build our theology over a single observation, it's clear that a life of faith is often a battle against fear.

The disciples discovered this lesson early on, when their boat was caught in a storm. Jesus, exhausted from the day, was asleep while His followers were frantic. When they finally woke Him, He rebuked not only the storm but the disciples as well:

And He got up and rebuked the wind and said to the sea,
"Hush, be still." And the wind died down and it became
perfectly calm. And He said to them, "Why are you afraid?
Do you still have no faith?" Mark 4:39-40 NASB

Fear certainly tested the faith of Jairus, the local synagogue leader in Mark chapter 5. In faith, he begged Jesus to come heal his sick daughter. Along the way, Jesus was delayed by an unexpected encounter with an ill woman who was healed instantly when she touched the hem of His clothes—a dramatic blessing for her but a seemingly catastrophic interruption for Jairus, who had placed all his hopes on Jesus reaching his daughter in time:

While [Jesus] was still speaking to [the woman who was healed],
messengers arrived from the home of Jairus, the leader of the
synagogue. They told him, "Your daughter is dead. There's
no use troubling the Teacher now." Mark 5:35 NLT

Jairus must have been in despair! His efforts had come so close! But Jesus, knowing the man's heart, quickly comforted him:

But Jesus overheard them and said to Jairus,
"Don't be afraid. Just have faith." Mark 5:36 NLT

Of course, we know that Jesus was going to raise the little girl back to life, but Jairus wasn't told how the story would end, just that he should choose faith over fear as they walked the rest of the way to his house where he knew that his daughter lay dead. That was literally a walk of faith!

But Jesus' teaching to move ahead in faith rather than shrink back in fear wasn't just for those times of extreme testing. It was for the daily fears and anxiety of life:

"But if God so clothes the grass of the field, which today is alive
and tomorrow is thrown into the oven, will he not much more
clothe you, O you of little faith?" Matthew 6:30 ESV

When we give in to fear, it means we're pulling back from God and His plans for us. Thankfully God does not leave us to fight the good fight of faith alone. We have an Advocate, a Helper, living within us who empowers us to face all fears:

For God has not given us a spirit of fear and timidity,
but of power, love, and self-discipline. 2 Timothy 1:7 NLT

We are called to move forward in faith as we keep in step with the Spirit within us. We may well wrestle with fear, but we are never alone in that struggle.

▶ What am I most afraid of? How am I handling it? Is it holding me back from growing in Christ or in any area of my life?

....

....

....

....

▶ What does the Bible have to say about the kind of things that make me afraid?

....

....

....

....

▶ How can I rely on the Holy Spirit more when fear tries to push me backward?

....

....

....

....

▶ Is there anyone I can share my fears with who will pray with me and for me?

....

....

....

MORNING

Ask the Lord for strength in battle against fear.

Something like this. . .

Father, You are with me always, and I pray that You will grant me the strength to face my fears with a heart of courage. Your faithfulness never fails, and I ask that when fear and anxiety threaten to overwhelm me, You help me stand against the tide, trusting in You to protect and watch over me.

....

....

....

....

....

....

....

....

....

....

....

....

AFTERNOON

Ask for God's peace to be upon you
during unsure and difficult times.

Something like this. . .

*Lord God, in Your mercy, cover me and my house with the
peace that passes all understanding. I pray against fear
of the future and ask that You instill within me the courage
to continue forward in faith, knowing that my needs will
be met and trusting in Your promises and plans.*

....

....

....

....

....

....

....

....

....

....

....

....

EVENING

Call out to Him for comfort when
you feel alone, isolated, and afraid.

Something like this. . .

*Father in heaven, rescue me from the darkness of isolation,
fear, and anxiety—I am covered under the sacrifice of Christ,
and fear has no power over me! I will never be alone, Lord,
for You are with me always. Thank You for Your everlasting
love and faithfulness, Almighty Father!*

DAY 8
SPIRITUALLY EFFECTIVE

For this very reason, make every effort to supplement
your faith with virtue, and virtue with knowledge,
and knowledge with self-control, and self-control
with steadfastness, and steadfastness with godliness,
and godliness with brotherly affection, and brotherly
affection with love. For if these qualities are yours
and are increasing, they keep you from being ineffective
or unfruitful in the knowledge of our Lord Jesus Christ.

2 PETER 1:5–8 ESV

Most men enjoy being good at something, whether it's a career, a sport, or
a hobby. We like the idea of being effective, of pursuing goals and achiev-
ing results—and being recognized for it! Additionally, most of us like to
be useful in our endeavors, producing something of value for ourselves
and others. It's in us by design: Adam's first job assignment was to tend a
garden. Something many of us still attempt each spring.

Not surprisingly, most men are willing to spend the time and energy
it takes to excel at their chosen task whether it requires education, cer-
tification, practice time, etc. But in spiritual work—the work that builds
the Kingdom of God—acquired skills are not the main concern, though
certainly they have an important place. King David was commended for
being just such a skilled leader:

With upright heart he shepherded them and
guided them with his skillful hand. Psalm 78:72 ESV

In addition to our natural skills and talents, God gives each of us spiritual gifts to be used to help the body of Christ grow, and we are to use them
responsibly:

Now there are varieties of gifts, but the same Spirit;
and there are varieties of service, but the same Lord;
and there are varieties of activities, but it is the same

God who empowers them all in everyone. To each
is given the manifestation of the Spirit for the
common good. 1 Corinthians 12:4-7 ESV

But real effectiveness in the Kingdom is not just a combination of acquired skills, natural talents, or even God-given gifts. True spiritual effectiveness, Peter says, is tied to the character of the worker. Peter points us to seven "qualities" that, when added to our faith, create a foundation for being useful and fruitful in God's work: virtue, knowledge, self-control, steadfastness, godliness, brotherly affection, and love. This list overlaps with Paul's description of the fruit of the Spirit in Galatians 5:22-23, but here Peter emphasizes the choice we have in these attitudes and values—these character traits. We may or may not possess them in any great degree. We have to make some effort to have them. Just as Adam tended the fruit of the Garden, we are responsible to tend the fruit of the Spirit.

And we aren't to be static in these qualities, but increasing in them, according to Peter. Then, from these internal qualities, right actions will come, just as from good soil good fruit will grow. Skills and gifts will truly find a good place to take root in character that is growing to be like Jesus.

The promise in today's verse is a grand one: we can't fail if we possess the qualities Peter identifies, because as we grow in Christlikeness we grow in spiritual effectiveness. No wonder Peter exhorts us to be diligent—"make every effort"—to add these qualities to our faith! These are character traits that will reflect Christ in every work He has called us to do.

▶ Do I see my efforts to walk with Christ and build His kingdom bearing fruit?

....

....

....

....

....

....

▶ What real efforts am I making to become more virtuous? More knowledgeable? More self-controlled? More steadfast? More godly? More loving toward other believers?

....

....

....

....

....

....

▶ How can I help my brothers in Christ grow in these traits?

....

....

....

....

....

....

MORNING

Ask God to reveal areas in your life that you could grow in.

Something like this. . .

Lord God, as I go about my day, reveal to me the qualities that I am lacking in so that I may grow to be more fruitful in Your kingdom. Help me to be diligent in increasing those qualities by taking every opportunity that You present to strengthen the foundation You've already laid in Christ.

....

....

....

....

....

....

....

....

....

....

....

....

....

AFTERNOON

Ask God for a heart of humbleness when working for
the Kingdom and growing with brothers in Christ.

Something like this. . .

*Lord, grant me a humble heart so that while I work to
increase my spiritual effectiveness for the Kingdom,
I attribute every result and success to You. In the
same way I pray that You will give me a heart of
service and brotherly affection when serving my
brothers in Christ along their journeys.*

EVENING

Thank God for the gifts He gives and ask for
His help in guiding you to grow in your faith.

Something like this. . .

*I praise You, Father, for the gifts and skills You bestow on us!
Thank You for working in my life to grow the qualities
necessary to become more effective for Your Kingdom.
I ask for Your guidance in growing my faith, so that fruitful
and good works would overflow as I make every
effort to increase in usefulness in Your hands.*

DAY 9
A GOOD MESS

Without oxen a stable stays clean,
but you need a strong ox for a large harvest.
PROVERBS 14:4 NLT

Oxen are powerful creatures with a history intertwined with human-kind. Their domestication as a draft animal is estimated to have started around 4000 BC. They're first mentioned in the Bible in Genesis 12, in a list of valuable gifts from Pharaoh to Abram. A healthy ox to pull a plow was expensive, and an evenly matched pair that pulled in unison was even more so. If you were able to afford such beasts, they most certainly multiplied the work you could accomplish and expanded your ability to plant and harvest crops.

However, owning an ox comes with a few consequences. They like to eat, they don't fit into small spaces, they smell bad, and they don't use a litterbox. But there's no way to take advantage of their amazing strength without having to watch where you step! That's a pretty good metaphor for life: If you want to produce something of value, you're going to have to deal with the mess that may be associated with it.

Marriage, for all its delights, can generate piles of debris. Sacrificing individual dreams, working through conflict, dealing with in-laws, negotiating finances, serving even when you would prefer to be served—all these make for a messy "stable." For those who persevere, however, the rewards are well worth it.

Having kids may be both figuratively and literally one of the messiest choices you can make in life. They eat messy, they do not know what a toilet is until you explain it (repeatedly), and they break your heart one way or another. But most parents would tell you they'd do it all over again without blinking an eye. The gain far exceeds the pain.

Some guys aren't married, and not every man will raise kids. Not a problem—the workplace demonstrates the principle of the messy stable quite adequately. It's risky to start a business, choose a career, take a promotion, or switch jobs. Sometimes you have to make the decision to move and leave friends and family or miss a great opportunity for advancement. Employees and coworkers don't always do what you expect or even what they promised, customers and bosses demand more than you can provide, every week you have to clean up something that hit the fan—even if it isn't your fault! But we take the mess because of the possibilities.

Being active in a Christ-centered congregation is essential but takes time, effort, and sacrifice. The strength of a good church is like that of an ox—producing far more as a whole than we can individually, even if the individuals aren't perfect. Sometimes, even at church, you will have to watch where you step!

The principle in this verse is that nothing of value comes without some unpleasant aspects: hard work, unpredictable consequences, and real risk. God wants us to work at whatever He's put into our lives, not fearing the consequences but focusing on creating something of value. It's complicated sometimes as we look at opportunities, so Paul exhorts us to meditate on this concept:

> *And athletes cannot win the prize unless they*
> *follow the rules. And hardworking farmers should*
> *be the first to enjoy the fruit of their labor. Think*
> *about what I am saying. The Lord will help you*
> *understand all these things. 2 Timothy 2:5-7 NLT*

As men, God has offered us possibilities, and we have to understand clearly that the mess that goes with our choices is also part of the deal. But He wouldn't invite us to greater things if it weren't in our best interest; and if everything were easy, we'd be no better men for it.

▶ Is there any arena of my life that I have mistakenly thought should come easy and without hard work and risk?

....

....

....

....

....

....

▶ What am I pursuing, working at, and sacrificing for currently? Do I understand that "success" in those areas might have some messy consequences?

....

....

....

....

....

....

▶ What has God called me to do that I might have been avoiding because I know there will be a real price to pay?

....

....

....

....

MORNING

Ask God for the drive to work hard in every area of your life.

Something like this. . .

Father, I pray that You give me a good attitude and drive to complete the work You've set before me, no matter how hard or taxing it is. Please give me patience and energy so that I may have the same hardworking attitude and self-discipline it takes to complete even greater works for Your kingdom.

....
....
....
....
....
....
....
....
....
....
....
....

AFTERNOON

Confess laziness or any fears holding you
back from what God has called you to do.

Something like this. . .

*Father, I confess that in some areas in my life, I often put
things off or make excuses because the work is "messy"
or I'm afraid of consequences. Lord, help me to overcome
laziness, anxiety, distraction, and fear, so that I may fully
embrace the tasks that You have laid before me.*

....

....

....

....

....

....

....

....

....

....

....

EVENING

Ask for His guidance in pursuing the right things and sacrificing for the right goals.

Something like this. . .

Lord Almighty, I ask for Your help and guidance when working hard toward my goals. Keep me on the path You've set for me, so that in everything I do, I honor You. I pray that selfish ambition and pride be stripped from me. Please grant me a heart of service like Jesus.

....
....
....
....
....
....
....
....
....
....
....
....

DAY 10
DOS AND DON'TS

> Then the LORD God took the man and put him into the garden of
> Eden to cultivate it and keep it. The LORD God commanded the
> man, saying, "From any tree of the garden you may eat freely; but
> from the tree of the knowledge of good and evil you shall not eat,
> for in the day that you eat from it you will surely die."
> GENESIS 2:15–17 NASB

Adam was designed to enjoy uninterrupted union with God and with the
world around him. He was without sin living in a garden planted by God
Himself. And he had only one restriction: don't eat of the fruit of the tree
of the knowledge of good and evil. And it wasn't an arbitrary commandment; it was for his own protection. God clearly explained to Adam why
He withheld that single fruit: it was the one thing that would end the union
he was created to enjoy and introduce death to the world. It was the only
"don't" in a world of "dos". . .for a while.

Eve had not yet been created when God told Adam not to eat of
that one tree. She came into existence just after that commandment
was given:

> Then the LORD God said, "It is not good for the man to be alone;
> I will make him a helper suitable for him." Genesis 2:18 NASB

And He sure did! Adam was delighted, and the couple was happy.
They had the same uninterrupted union Adam enjoyed with God (Genesis
2:23-25). Adam, being a good husband, explained the commandment he
had received from God and apparently added one addition of his own:

> The woman said to the serpent, "From the fruit of the trees of
> the garden we may eat; but from the fruit of the tree which is
> in the middle of the garden, God has said, 'You shall not eat
> from it or touch it, or you will die.' " Genesis 3:2-3 NASB

Adam was a good husband, reflecting God's desire to shield the one he
loved from destruction. And as Eve's authority, Adam had the right to add

his own "don't" to protect her. But of course, we all know that two "don'ts" still didn't work:

> *She saw that the tree was beautiful and its fruit looked delicious, and she wanted the wisdom it would give her. So she took some of the fruit and ate it. Then she gave some to her husband, who was with her, and he ate it, too.* Genesis 3:6 NLT

It's interesting to note that although Eve disobeyed two "don'ts" (touching and eating), the consequences of their actions only occurred after Adam ate the fruit. He was the one ultimately charged with the responsibility for obedience. He failed to protect his wife, his own soul, and his offspring, passing on the tendency to ignore God to all generations that followed. His one act of disobedience multiplied into all the variety of things we call sin today. No wonder the "don'ts" seem to multiply throughout the Bible. . . they're just keeping pace with the ways man has invented to disregard God!

Some people dismiss the Bible as a mere collection of rules and restrictions and miss the original purpose of God's "don'ts." He wanted to keep us in fellowship with Himself, with one another, and with the world around us, to protect us from self-destruction. Even the Old Testament Law with all its prohibitions and regulations was a gift to protect His people—a gift to increase their joy, not end it—and ultimately to lead people to Christ:

> *The law was our guardian until Christ came; it protected us until we could be made right with God through faith.* Galatians 3:24 NLT

Now, having been made right with God through and in Jesus Christ, the "don'ts" from God aren't a law carrying some heavy penalty—they provide real freedom and create a holy experience with our Lord. In Christ, any "don't" from our Father means life and peace for us.

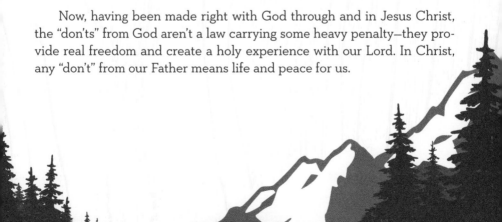

▶ Is there any area of my life or thinking where God says "don't" but that I've been doing anyway?

....

....

....

....

....

....

▶ Which of God's commandments do I see as hard or restrictive rather than freeing and protective?

....

....

....

....

....

....

▶ Is there anyone in my life whom I'm responsible to protect? How could I do a better job?

....

....

....

....

....

....

MORNING

**Ask the Lord to help you let go of the areas
in your life that are self-destructive.**

Something like this...

*Father, I ask Your forgiveness for clinging to the things
in my life that I know are self-destructive, despite Your
commands. I submit it all to You. You bring joy and peace,
and I want to revel in the freedom that only You can
provide. Lord, please free me from any bondage that I
create for myself, and grant me the strength and discipline
to face these areas in my life and let them go.*

....

....

....

....

....

....

....

....

....

....

AFTERNOON

Ask God to change your attitude to one that sees
His commands as protective, not restrictive.

Something like this. . .

*Lord Almighty, I confess that I often struggle with a selfish
and rebellious attitude when it comes to keeping Your
commandments. Shape my heart into one that understands
the freedom You offer us through the rules You provide.
I thank You, Father, for the commandments
that keep me in fellowship with You!*

....

....

....

....

....

....

....

....

....

....

....

....

EVENING

Ask the Father to help you better protect those whom you are responsible for.

Something like this. . .

Lord, please help me to be a better servant and shield to those whom I am responsible for protecting. I ask that You please help me not to "abandon my post" when tempted by the offerings of the world but that I would instead stand strong with courage and loyalty—so that through the keeping of your commandments, I can protect the ones I love from harm.

DAY 11
PRIDE

As he looked out across the city, he said, "Look at this great city
of Babylon! By my own mighty power, I have built this beautiful
city as my royal residence to display my majestic splendor." While
these words were still in his mouth, a voice called down from
heaven, "O King Nebuchadnezzar, this message is for you! You are
no longer ruler of this kingdom. You will be driven from human
society. You will live in the fields with the wild animals, and you
will eat grass like a cow. Seven periods of time will pass while you
live this way, until you learn that the Most High rules over the
kingdoms of the world and gives them to anyone he chooses."
DANIEL 4:30-32 NLT

Success and achievement are great—unless they lead you to forget basic
spiritual truths. Truths like: you cannot really accomplish anything apart
from God. He is the Most High, and no matter how much we may achieve
on earth, our success is ultimately His gift. It's given for His purposes,
not for our boasting. In fact, we can't even earn a basic living without
God, as Moses pointed out to the people as they were about to enter the
promised land:

In the wilderness He fed you manna which your fathers
did not know, that He might humble you and that He might
test you, to do good for you in the end. Otherwise, you may
say in your heart, "My power and the strength of my hand
made me this wealth." But you shall remember the LORD your
God, for it is He who is giving you power to make wealth,
that He may confirm His covenant which He swore to your
fathers, as it is this day. Deuteronomy 8:16-18 NASB

We exist in an economy of God's design, and our careers, our work,
our paycheck—all our activities—are a gift from Him. James reminds
believers, as Moses did, that the future belongs to God, and that worldly
success is in His hands:

Come now, you who say, "Today or tomorrow we will go into such and such a town and spend a year there and trade and make a profit"—yet you do not know what tomorrow will bring. What is your life? For you are a mist that appears for a little time and then vanishes. Instead you ought to say, "If the Lord wills, we will live and do this or that." As it is, you boast in your arrogance. All such boasting is evil. James 4:13-16 ESV

How easy and natural it feels to take credit for our own success! But it's a fool's game. That's the lesson in the cautionary tale of Nebuchadnezzar: arrogance always invites correction. As the apostle Peter said,

"GOD IS OPPOSED TO THE PROUD, BUT GIVES GRACE TO THE HUMBLE." 1 Peter 5:5 NASB

God, the Source of All Things, doesn't simply ignore the proud or just work around them—He actively opposes them. Perhaps you think of the "proud" as those who dismiss God's existence or scoff at religion. Surely, they qualify, but when we as believers, knowing Christ, are tempted to pat ourselves on the back we should take note, as Nebuchadnezzar eventually did, that we are giving credit to the wrong person. And you don't have to be some obnoxious "overachiever" to get God's attention! Anyone who takes credit for what God has done can enjoy the blessing of His painful mercy and His loving correction. God rebukes the foolishness of the high and low alike, because He is merciful to all.

▶ What things have I accomplished that I really enjoy being recognized for? Do I ever bring them up in conversation so I can talk about them? Why?

....
....
....
....
....
....

▶ Has God ever pulled the rug out from under me to help me see Him better?

....
....
....
....
....
....

▶ If I were to list all my true achievements in life, could I also describe how God worked in each one of them for His glory?

....
....
....
....
....

MORNING

Ask God to help keep you humble through His just correction, so you may rejoice in the gifts He gives.

Something like this. . .

Father, in Your loving mercy, correct my prideful and boastful ways. I ask that You mold me into a man who's humble and thankful for every success, large or small. Help me to take a godly approach to the achievements in my life so that I may take pleasure only in honoring You, with thanksgiving.

....

....

....

....

....

....

....

....

....

....

....

....

AFTERNOON

Praise God for the times when He has "pulled the rug out from under you" in order to help you see Him better, and let go of anger and resentment.

Something like this. . .

Almighty God, thank You for teaching me to see more clearly, even when the lesson seems harsh. I surrender and ask Your forgiveness for any anger or resentment that I have held on to. Please continue to teach me, Lord, and instill within me a trust to follow Your will, rather than attempt to achieve anything on my own.

....

....

....

....

....

....

....

....

....

....

EVENING

**Ask the Lord to help you overcome using your
achievements in conflict and jealousy of others' success.**

Something like this. . .

*Lord, I confess I show off my achievements to one-up
others or prove my value. I also allow jealousy and
resentment of others' success to distract me. Father,
free me from this arrogance! I ask that You would replace
my prideful attitude with one that is full of grace, love,
and earnest excitement for others, giving all glory to You.*

DAY 12
SEXUALITY, PART 1

"Therefore a man shall leave his father and mother and hold fast to his wife, and the two shall become one flesh." This mystery is profound, and I am saying that it refers to Christ and the church.
EPHESIANS 5:31–32 ESV

It's no surprise that we live in a nation and a time that is obsessed with sexuality. In the aftermath of the so-called "sexual revolution" of the 1960s, sex moved from the realm of the private to the realm of entertainment. Monogamy was suddenly "old-fashioned" in the age of "free love." Pornography got shortened to "porn" as if giving a disease a nickname would make it less deadly.

The results are well documented: increased sexual activity among teens, venereal disease, abortion, divorce, and addiction to pornography. This "revolution" led not to more freedom but to more enslavement and confusion.

The authors of the New Testament knew what it was to live in a twisted world, surrounded by Roman and Greek pagan values. Today we must be clear on God's plans and expectations for sex too, keeping a biblical perspective.

Marriage is to portray the intimacy Christ plans for His Bride.

"This mystery is profound" to say the least: marriage, consummated righteously, was designed to be a testimony of the plan God will reveal in the fullness of time. Christ wants unity with His people the way a loving, respectful man desires oneness with his wife.

Sex within marriage fosters unity.

> He answered, "Have you not read that he who created them
> from the beginning made them male and female, and said,
> 'Therefore a man shall leave his father and his mother and hold
> fast to his wife, and the two shall become one flesh'? So they
> are no longer two but one flesh." Matthew 19:4-6 ESV

God's plan from the beginning for marriage was oneness. A sacred oneness that is beyond separation and can be metaphorically represented by the birth of a child—the two beings blended into one person.

Marriage should be honored by society, not treated lightly.

Let marriage be held in honor among all. Hebrews 13:4 ESV

Any marriage that is legitimately entered into by a man and a woman should be considered inviolable, particularly among believers.

Sex in marriage should not be mixed with the world's perspective.

Let the marriage bed be undefiled, for God will judge the sexually immoral and adulterous. Hebrews 13:4 ESV

A godly husband should literally ask WWJD in bed? Selfishness is un-Christlike, but in the marriage bed it's particularly destructive. Giving should characterize the attitude of a respectful husband, not getting.

Sexual misconduct is a heart issue, not a physical issue.

For out of the heart come evil thoughts, murder, adultery, sexual immorality, theft, false witness, slander. Matthew 15:19 ESV

Sin is birthed from within. But Jesus is making us new from the inside out by His Holy Spirit. This is the starting point for real change in our sexual understanding and behavior.

Ultimately, our bodies do not even belong to us.

Or do you not know that your body is a temple of the Holy Spirit who is in you, whom you have from God, and that you are not your own? For you have been bought with a price: therefore glorify God in your body. 1 Corinthians 6:19-20 NASB

Believers do not have the right to misuse their bodies. It's Someone else's property.

There's a design and purpose for our sexuality that is transcendent. Marriage is the context for its healthy expression, a living metaphor for the mystery of Christ and the church. Within the context of a healthy marriage, sex is far more than a physical delight—it's a spiritual expression, honoring God and testifying to the truth of His plan.

▶ Is there anything in my heart or mind that contaminates the marriage bed?

....

....

....

....

▶ Do I protect my wife by being unselfish sexually? Or am I impatient and demanding about sex?

....

....

....

....

▶ How would I express God's perspective on the righteous design for sex to someone unfamiliar with the Bible?

....

....

....

....

▶ Is there anything I need to repent of or confess to someone I trust?

....

....

....

....

MORNING

Confess any strongholds of sexual immorality you have allowed in your life, and ask God for cleansing.

Something like this. . .

Holy Father, I call to You to ask for Your forgiveness. I have allowed the world to infect my understanding of intimacy and sex, and in doing so, allowed lust and immorality to find a place in my heart. In Your mercy, cleanse me from within, so that the overflow of my heart would be honoring to You always.

AFTERNOON

Whether married or not, ask the Lord to help guide and shape you in becoming the man you need to be in all relationships.

Something like this. . .

Good Father, I ask that You guide me when I am lost in the maze of lust and immoral thoughts. Please give me the strength and wisdom to see the ways out that You always provide. Father, I pray that You will guide and change me into a man full of patience, understanding, and gentleness, so that my heart is free from selfish and demanding desires, and so I can protect the sanctity of all relationships.

....

....

....

....

....

....

....

....

....

....

....

....

EVENING

Ask the Lord to strengthen you when you're
faced with opportunities for immorality.

Something like this. . .

*Almighty God, I call to You because I am often being
attacked by sexual temptation. Guard my heart against
the enemy that wants to see me destroyed. You are within
me Lord, and I can do all things through the strength You
provide. Please help me clear my mind, and I pray for Your
holiness to fill me, that I may stand firm in Christ.*

....

....

....

....

....

....

....

....

....

....

....

DAY 13
SEXUALITY, PART 2

*For this is the will of God, your sanctification: that you abstain
from sexual immorality; that each one of you know how
to control his own body in holiness and honor*
1 THESSALONIANS 4:3-6 ESV

Understanding God's plan has for marriage is the beginning of a healthy view of our sexuality. But it's not complete without a plan to avoid immorality. God asks us to "make no provision for the flesh in regard to its lusts" (Romans 13:14 NASB).

To put it bluntly, we can't afford to live life without a plan to keep ourselves from the traps of lust, pornography, fornication, and adultery.

*A prudent person foresees danger and takes
precautions. The simpleton goes blindly on
and suffers the consequences. Proverbs 27:12 NLT*

So, what does a plan of action to avoid immorality look like?

We need to establish a sense of urgency.

*Beloved, I urge you as aliens and strangers to abstain from fleshly
lusts which wage war against the soul. 1 Peter 2:11 NASB*

We're talking about warfare. This is not something that can be approached casually. Even if we didn't have an active enemy—which we do—our own flesh, our connection to this world, isn't doing us any favors. In this struggle, we need the help of like-minded men with whom we can partner for the protection of loving but brutally honest accountability.

An utter commitment to honoring Christ whatever the costs—married or single.

"You have heard that it was said, 'You shall not commit adultery.' But I say to you that everyone who looks at a woman with lustful intent has already committed adultery with her in his heart. If your right eye causes you to sin, tear it out and throw it away. For it is better that you lose one of your members than that your whole body be thrown into hell." Matthew 5:27-29 ESV

Jesus is employing hyperbole here for effect: sexual sin is like a spreading disease, and amputation is better than total devastation.

Being continually filled with the right things leaves less room for the wrong things.

> *But I say, walk by the Spirit, and you will not gratify the desires of the flesh. Galatians 5:16 ESV*

We leave no place for what is fake when we are filled with what is true. God's Word and prayer should be like a banquet that our minds are feasting on, not nibbling at. Our thought life must camp on what is righteous and spiritually healthy:

> *Whatever is true, whatever is honorable, whatever is right, whatever is pure, whatever is lovely, whatever is of good repute, if there is any excellence and if anything worthy of praise, dwell on these things. Philippians 4:8 NASB*

Use some godly common sense.

> *And I have seen among the simple, I have perceived among the youths, a young man lacking sense, passing along the street near her corner [the adulteress], taking the road to her house in the twilight, in the evening, at the time of night and darkness. Proverbs 7:7–9 ESV*

We can't afford to wander around in areas of life that we know will be a problem. Not a man alive can go toe-to-toe with sexual temptation for long and win. We know better than to linger in tempting situations online or at work or in our neighborhoods or at home or on business trips. Most of us know where and when the real problems are before we head into them.

Be prepared to run away!

> *Flee from sexual immorality. Every other sin a person commits is outside the body, but the sexually immoral person sins against his own body. 1 Corinthians 6:18 ESV*

We have to put whatever distance it takes between ourselves and sexual sin. If we are to honor God we must run toward Him.

▶ Do I really believe that sexual sin is as serious as the biblical writers did? Have I made excuses about my thinking or behavior?

....
....
....
....

▶ Do I have any sexual habit that I would be embarrassed to talk about even to a trusted friend or counselor?

....
....
....
....

▶ Am I being naive by spending too much time online or watching illicit shows? Am I spending too much time with the wrong person or people?

....
....
....
....

▶ Am I filling my mind and heart with the right kinds of things?

....
....
....
....

MORNING

Ask God to guide you in setting up safeguards against temptations.

Something like this. . .

Almighty Father, please forgive me when I allow my defenses to stagnate or ignorantly think I am capable of handling these temptations on my own. I cannot fight this war without You, Lord. Guide me in setting up stronger safeguards in my life, so that I may be truly ready for the battles that come.

....
....
....
....
....
....
....
....
....
....
....

AFTERNOON

Confess to Him what you may be too embarrassed
to confess to anyone else, asking for His
forgiveness and trusting in His faithfulness.

Something like this. . .

*Father, I confess to You my struggles with lust, pornography,
and sexually immoral thoughts, allowing them all to linger like
a disease, and I often find myself repeating the same mistakes
over and over. I thank You for Your faithfulness and mercy in
loving me despite the decisions I make. Deliver me from the
hold these things have on my thoughts and my life, and help
me destroy any excuses I create to continue in these cycles.*

EVENING

Ask God to give you a heart that seeks to know
His Word so that your mind is filled with good things.

Something like this. . .

*Lord, I confess that sometimes I would rather enjoy worldly
distractions than spend time in Your Word. I also confess
that at the same time I selfishly question why I "don't have
answers," despite the fact that You've already provided them
in Your Word! Forgive my ignorance and replace it with an
overwhelming hunger to feast on what You've written.*

DAY 14
GROWING UP

And I, brethren, could not speak to you as to spiritual men,
but as to men of flesh, as to infants in Christ. I gave you milk
to drink, not solid food; for you were not yet able to receive it.
Indeed, even now you are not yet able, for you are still fleshly.
1 CORINTHIANS 3:1–3 NASB

Do you remember the moment you first realized you weren't a kid anymore? Maybe it was something small like getting your first paycheck or your driver's license. Maybe it was a major life transition like graduating high school or moving out on your own. Perhaps it was a time of hardship like losing a parent or a life-threatening illness. Whatever your moment or season was, all men know that at some point boyhood is coming to a close and manhood has begun.

Growth is what we were designed for; growing up is good. Even Jesus experienced growing into manhood. Luke gives us two interesting incidents about Jesus' early life. From the time of His circumcision at eight days old until Jesus was twelve, Luke sums up His early childhood in a single statement:

The Child continued to grow and become strong, increasing in wisdom; and the grace of God was upon Him. Luke 2:40 NASB

When Jesus was twelve years old, His parents took Him to Jerusalem for the Passover. But when they left to return home, Jesus stayed behind. Assuming He was with relatives in the caravan, Joseph and Mary didn't discover their mistake for a full day. They returned to Jerusalem and searched for three more days. When they found Jesus in the temple listening to and asking questions of the rabbis, He seemed surprised it took them so long to figure out where He was:

"But why did you need to search?" he asked. "Didn't you know that I must be in my Father's house?" Luke 2:49 NLT

With this incident, Jesus made it known whose Son He was. He was no longer Joseph and Mary's little boy—He was growing into manhood according to God's plan:

"And Jesus kept increasing in wisdom and stature,
and in favor with God and men." Luke 2:52 NASB

Our spiritual maturity as believers is intended to follow the same pattern Jesus experienced. We are to increase in godly understanding and spiritual stature. Paul's lament to the Corinthian church in today's verse was that they had languished in spiritual infancy rather than grown up to become "spiritual men." They displayed none of the signs of adulthood in their faith. Like kids, these people were jealous, quarrelsome, captive to their emotions, boastful, lacking self-control, and did not properly understand the scriptures—much to Paul's annoyance! It was well past time for them to do what Paul himself had done:

When I was a child, I spoke and thought and
reasoned as a child. But when I grew up, I put
away childish things. 1 Corinthians 13:11 NLT

The writer of Hebrews lodged a very similar complaint toward the stubbornly immature readers of his letter:

You have been believers so long now that you ought to
be teaching others. Instead, you need someone to teach
you again the basic things about God's word. You are like
babies who need milk and cannot eat solid food. For someone
who lives on milk is still an infant and doesn't know how to
do what is right. Solid food is for those who are mature, who
through training have the skill to recognize the difference
between right and wrong. Hebrews 5:12-14 NLT

If we act like little boys in regard to our faith, rather than men, we are denying the very destiny we were born into by God's Spirit. God's intention is to have children, yes, but grown ones, in the image of His Son (Romans 8:29). We need to be intentional, studying our Father's Word, praying for His guidance, sharing our struggles with brothers who want the same for their lives, and telling everyone around us about His love and great promises. Those are the things that grown men do and that this world needs.

▶ What evidence can I point to in my own life that I am growing in Christ?

....
....
....
....

▶ Have I become complacent or lax in any spiritual discipline that I used to pursue?

....
....
....
....

▶ How can I grow in wisdom that will help other men become more like Jesus?

....
....
....
....

▶ Am I supposed to be teaching the things of God by now? How can I begin?

....
....
....
....

MORNING

Ask God for the wisdom to increase your growth in Christ.

Something like this. . .

Father, grant me the wisdom and understanding to overcome my spiritual infancy, so I may keep growing in You and Your Word. Father, please guide me to be more Christlike and bring me into spiritual maturity so that I may be a man who can better serve Your Kingdom.

AFTERNOON

Pray against distraction and complacency in your spiritual life.

Something like this. . .

*Almighty Father, I pray that You will aid me in my struggle
against distraction and stagnation. I ask that You would
help me hone my spiritual focus and sweep aside the laziness
and inaction I have allowed into my spiritual walk with You.
Forgive me for being complacent and for making excuses.
Please renew my energy to know You.*

....
....
....
....
....
....
....
....
....
....
....
....

EVENING

Ask the Lord for a humble heart during your spiritual growth and for wisdom when helping or teaching others.

Something like this. . .

Father, please reveal to me the areas where I need to grow and mature so I can help guide and teach others when needed. I ask also for a humble and gentle heart that is honoring to You. I pray against the self-righteousness and pride that can often overtake those in a teaching or mentoring position. I ask that You hold me accountable in remembering that we are all growing in You together.

....

....

....

....

....

....

....

....

....

....

....

DAY 15
COMMUNITY

Let us hold tightly without wavering to the hope we affirm,
for God can be trusted to keep his promise. Let us think
of ways to motivate one another to acts of love and good
works. And let us not neglect our meeting together, as
some people do, but encourage one another, especially
now that the day of his return is drawing near.
HEBREWS 10:23–25 NLT

It's a well-documented fact that men do not form as many deep relationships with other men as they used to. Over the last century, particularly
in America, men sharing their time and their emotions with other men
has grown less and less popular. Societal changes from the Industrial
Revolution to the increased mobility allowed by the automobile began
to change the marketplace, offering better jobs in more urban areas. Men
moved away from the friendships they developed growing up on farms
and in small communities, opting for cities where career opportunities
were abundant.

Coupled with this phenomenon was the growing focus of the mid-
dle class on the nuclear family. Men simply ran out of time, and deep
friendships with other men was the first thing to go. Sure, we all have
buddies, but most often these relationships are formed around school,
work, or sports with no guarantee of depth, much less meaningful
engagement. These are friends that *Boston Globe* writer Billy Baker
calls, "accidents of proximity."

Even the church can be a superficial place for men. Whether we
stay anonymous, nodding to men whose names we don't know, or busy
ourselves doing the things that keep the church in operation, it's just as
easy to miss out on spiritual encouragement at church as at the com-
pany softball game.

This may be the culture we were all born into, but it's not what we
have to accept. God established the church as the "body of Christ"—a
living identity for us all:

*Just as our bodies have many parts and each part
has a special function, so it is with Christ's body.
We are many parts of one body, and we all
belong to each other. Romans 12:4-5 NLT*

We were called into a unique kind of fellowship; we actually belong to one another. We are to drop any cultural differences, macho reservation, or Christian facade and be vulnerable and real. We are to open up courageously and accept others unconditionally. We are to be committed to each other in all humility and with real intentionality:

*Be devoted to one another in brotherly love;
give preference to one another in honor; not
lagging behind in diligence, fervent in spirit,
serving the Lord. Romans 12:10-11 NASB*

It is the Lord Himself we serve when we serve our brothers, and it's His law we fulfill when we expend ourselves in service to any of His people:

*Bear one another's burdens, and thereby
fulfill the law of Christ. Galatians 6:2 NASB*

Being a part of a "good church" is just the beginning. The assembly we choose needs us as much as we need them, which is why we can't neglect meeting together. Isolation is the enemy of intimacy. Relationships require time, effort, and thought; we have to plan and work to build and maintain them, because other men are just as busy and distracted as we are! We have to "think of ways to motivate one another" rather than assuming it just happens whenever we cross paths.

▶ What is the best male relationship I have? Does it encourage me spiritually?

....

....

....

....

▶ Am I involved with any group of men with whom I could share my deepest fears and greatest failures?

....

....

....

....

▶ Is my church a place where men are connecting and growing, and am I a part of that?

....

....

....

....

▶ What can I do to begin building relationships that would inspire me and others to live more completely for Christ?

....

....

....

....

MORNING

Ask God to reveal the ways you can be encouraging to your brothers in Christ.

Something like this. . .

Father, as I go about my day, I ask that You reveal to me the ways in which I can encourage and motivate my friends and brothers in Christ in their spiritual walk. Give me the wisdom, strength, and discernment to help them shoulder any burdens that weigh on or isolate them so that we may all grow closer as brothers serving in Your Kingdom.

AFTERNOON

Ask God for help in being vulnerable
to fellow brothers in Christ.

Something like this. . .

*In You, Lord, I find my identity, not in the shallow facade that
is worldly masculinity. And so, I confess that I have often been
reserved in my willingness to open up to the men I have built
friendships with, either out of fear or pride. Lord, help me to
have the courage to be able to speak about my burdens, fears,
and pains, as well as when I stumble and need accountability
partners to help bring me back onto a path that honors You.*

EVENING

Go to your heavenly Father for strength in times when you feel isolated, and ask Him for opportunities to build deep friendships or further the friendships you have.

Something like this. . .

Lord, I know that when I am alone, You are still with me. When I feel the darkness of isolation, I know You are my comfort and strength. Father, guide me and give me courage to build godly relationships, strengthen friendships, and find fellowship that inspires me to increasingly and wholeheartedly glorify You.

DAY 16
NOT PERFECT, JUST CALLED

For the foolishness of God is wiser than men, and the weakness
of God is stronger than men. For consider your calling, brothers:
not many of you were wise according to worldly standards, not
many were powerful, not many were of noble birth. But God chose
what is foolish in the world to shame the wise; God chose
what is weak in the world to shame the strong.
1 CORINTHIANS 1:25–27 ESV

If you look at the leaders of the Bible you will see a disturbing pattern: they don't fit any pattern! You have shepherds, slaves, fishermen, orphans, princes, nomads, soldiers; some are eloquent; some are tongue-tied; some were moral; many had epic frailties, people of questionable skills and dubious choices. They fit no practical profile.

Consider Noah. He led his family into salvation by building an enormous, seemingly useless boat. He was willing to fall on his face before a wicked world if God didn't follow through on what He had promised. And God did follow through, yet Noah ultimately ended up drunk, naked, and cursing one of his own sons (Genesis 9:20–25). And pretty soon all his descendants were just as bad as the group he left behind to tread water.

Moses, a stammerer, a prince, a murderer and fugitive, spent more than forty years being second-guessed by a bunch of stiff-necked, ignorant, grumbling Israelites and finally died on the wrong side of the Jordan because he dishonored God in front of everyone (Deuteronomy 34:5).

Abraham, the man God chose as His covenant partner, had an illegitimate son whom he sent packing, along with his mother, into the desert to fend for themselves (Genesis 21:14). His son Isaac, through whom God would fulfill His promise, created animosity in his own family by favoring his elder son, Esau, over the younger son, Jacob (Genesis 25:28). Jacob—whose willingness to wrestle a blessing from God would later earn him the name Israel (Genesis 35:10)—was, for most of his life, a liar and a cheat. Like his father, he engendered murderous jealously within his family by favoring one son over the others (Genesis 37:4).

King David, the songwriter, the brigand, the murderer, the adulterer, and a man after God's own heart (Acts 13:22), suffered the split of his family and his kingdom, ending in the death of his usurper son, Absalom, who murdered the half-brother who had raped his sister (2 Samuel 13-18). David may have been a great leader of Israel, but he was a failed leader of his own household.

Solomon, who built the temple of God, had no excuse for his failings. Enlightened by God beyond anyone who had ever lived, he proceeded to violate the written warnings of Moses by collecting foreign wives who did exactly as predicted—they turned his heart from God (Deuteronomy 17:16-17). His wisdom was legendary, but his legacy was a disaster—a kingdom split in half after he died (1 Kings 11:11).

The New Testament has fewer examples since it covers a much shorter timeframe, but consider Peter, who had a personal relationship with Christ beyond anything we mean by that phrase today. He stepped out of the boat at Jesus' command (Matthew 14:29), he confessed Christ as Messiah (Mark 8:29), he saw his mother-in-law and many others healed (Luke 4:39), and he attacked the men who came to arrest Jesus (John 18:10). But he also denied Christ (Matthew 26:74) and was rebuked publicly for his blatant hypocrisy by Paul—a guy who never actually met the Messiah—years after leading the church (Galatians 2:11).

Although there's no consistent pattern to God's chosen men, there is a common thread: they all stepped out in faith. There were no guarantees of success and plenty of opportunities to fail publicly—and have their weaknesses apparent to all. Very often they were faithful failures, weak and inconsistent, but still useful in God's hands. If they were afraid or unworthy or ill-equipped, they still took a step of faith. They engaged with God, because He invited them into His kingdom, not because they were worthy of it.

When God calls us to follow Him and to lead others, He does so clearly understanding the men we are. He wants to use us while He changes us. No one has it all together but Christ alone.

▶ Have I ever resisted taking a step of faith because I felt unworthy or ill-prepared?

....

....

....

....

▶ Has fear of public failure ever caused me to avoid something I felt God was asking me to do?

....

....

....

....

▶ Where have I stepped out in faith and, despite my own shortcomings, seen God honor my efforts?

....

....

....

....

▶ Is there anything He's asking me to do right now that I might be making excuses to avoid?

....

....

....

....

MORNING

Ask the Father for courage and strength to
face the fear of public failure and judgment.

Something like this. . .

*Father, I confess that I have often been hesitant in doing
what You've asked of me because of the fear of public failure
or humiliation. I ask for Your forgiveness and that You would
grant me the courage and strength to wholeheartedly pursue
the tasks You've set before me, regardless of what anyone
may think. I live for You, Lord, not for anyone else's opinion.*

AFTERNOON

Ask God to aid you in times where you
feel unworthy or undeserving.

Something like this. . .

*Almighty Savior, please bring comfort and peace to my
mind when I feel worthless or undeserving of Your love.
Thank You for loving me despite my imperfections, and
please help remind me in the darkest times of self-doubt
that my worth comes from You, so that I may step forward
in faith and walk according to Your plan for my life.*

....

....

....

....

....

....

....

....

....

....

....

EVENING

Ask the Lord to open your eyes to see the opportunities He provides for taking steps of faith.

Something like this. . .

Father, I often find myself trapped within the confines of my own comfort zone, either too lazy, blind, or fearful to step outside its boundaries. In Your loving mercy, open my eyes to see the opportunities that You've placed before me. Help me see and take the steps of faith that You provide, trusting fully in You to guide and change me into a man who chases constantly after growth and faithfulness in You.

....
....
....
....
....
....
....
....
....
....

DAY 17
HARDENING OF THE HEART

> Let us not lose heart in doing good, for in due time we
> will reap if we do not grow weary. So then, while we have
> opportunity, let us do good to all people, and especially
> to those who are of the household of the faith.
> GALATIANS 6:9–10 NASB

In the movie *Raiders of the Lost Ark*, when Marion says to Indiana Jones, "You're not the man I knew ten years ago," he responds in his charming but patronizing way: "It's not the years, honey. It's the mileage."

That's a pretty accurate description of how the heart gets hardened. It's not necessarily a feature of age. The mileage of this world can be harsh for the young as well as the aged: failed relationships, unfulfilling careers, missed opportunities, maybe even catastrophic mistakes. Disappointments can lead to cynicism and a feeling of pointlessness, even hopelessness.

Solomon, the wisest king in history, summed up his worldly experiences in a book that could be called the Book of Disappointments:

> *I devoted myself to search for understanding and
> to explore by wisdom everything being done under
> heaven. I soon discovered that God has dealt a tragic exis-
> tence to the human race. I observed everything going
> on under the sun, and really, it is all meaningless—
> like chasing the wind. Ecclesiastes 1:13–14 NLT*

Solomon tested all the things this world had to offer to find meaning—achievement, glory, love, wisdom—and came up with a conclusion he repeated over and over: it's all in vain! A massive waste of time; a monumental disappointment. Without God, everything amounts to nothing.

Even those of us who know Christ and live for Him can grow weary and become discouraged. Jesus' own disciples experienced a hardening of heart when He was crucified. They had been hoping for the Son of David to usher in an earthly kingdom. After Jesus died, they wallowed in unbelief even though they had received credible reports of His resurrection:

*Afterward He appeared to the eleven themselves as
they were reclining at the table; and He reproached
them for their unbelief and hardness of heart, because
they had not believed those who had seen Him
after He had risen. Mark 16:14 NASB*

Their disappointment had quickly turned into cynicism even in the face of Jesus' promises and the testimony of witnesses. Growing weary in our faith makes us less responsive to the truth and more impatient with those who are living by faith, less willing to serve and more vulnerable to sin. And sin will take advantage of every opportunity we allow it. That's why we need loving accountability:

*You must warn each other every day, while it is still
"today," so that none of you will be deceived by
sin and hardened against God. Hebrews 3:13 NLT*

It takes courage to keep believing when the harvest we hope for seems far away, but that's why we are called to be part of a "household of the faith" and not go at the Christian life as a solo act. The world is "together" in its opposition to us, to wear us down and make us give up the good fight. We as the body of Christ need to look to the Head for our encouragement:

*For consider Him who has endured such hostility
by sinners against Himself, so that you will not
grow weary and lose heart. Hebrews 12:3 NASB*

Remaining open to God moment by moment, without a "plan B," takes courage. Living in accountable community where we serve one another takes commitment. Avoiding hardness in our thinking and coldness in our hearts takes humility. But we have a great Savior and His promise that, in time, a harvest will be ours.

▶ Where am I being tempted to become cynical or hardened?

....

....

....

....

▶ Have I let any area of my spiritual life become stagnant or dry?

....

....

....

....

▶ Do I help my fellow believers by encouraging them regularly to keep doing good and not lose heart?

....

....

....

....

....

▶ Whom can I partner with to keep pressing on in faith?

....

....

....

....

MORNING

Pray for strength and courage when faced with cynicism and doubt.

Something like this. . .

Father, provide the courage and strength I need to face the cynical and stagnant mind-set of the world. I ask that when I am tempted with worldly weariness that You grant me peace of mind, so that in my own selfishness, I do not harden my heart to Your loving plans for my life.

AFTERNOON

Confess the areas in your life where you have allowed your heart to harden and ask Him to change your heart to one of service.

Something like this. . .

God, I confess to You that I have allowed my heart to be hardened in many areas of my life. Forgive me, Father, and soften my heart to be more receptive to the hope You bring. Work in me to change any cynicism I have from the things I've experienced into sources of wisdom and encouragement that I can draw from to aid those around me to not lose hope.

....

....

....

....

....

....

....

....

....

....

....

....

EVENING

Ask God to heal you from trauma, guilt, anger, pain, or anything else that would harden your heart.

Something like this. . .

Father, I have made so many mistakes, and I've been through some painful experiences that have caused me to withdraw. Father, only You can bring healing, so I ask that You cleanse me with the peace of Your Son, Jesus. Please open my heart and allow me to be vulnerable and loving, despite being angry or hurt, so that I may honor You.

DAY 18
GRATITUDE

Then one of them, when he saw that he was healed, turned back,
praising God with a loud voice; and he fell on his face at Jesus'
feet, giving him thanks. Now he was a Samaritan. Then Jesus
answered, "Were not ten cleansed? Where are the nine? Was no
one found to return and give praise to God except this foreigner?"
LUKE 17:15–18 ESV

The rarest of all human traits is gratitude. In today's passage we can see
that demonstrated using actual numerical values! One out of ten lepers
healed of the wasting disease that isolated them from society thought to
pause and give thanks to Jesus. And he wasn't even an Israelite whose
hope was in a promised Messiah. Perhaps the others felt grateful, but
their expression of it was absent.

Honoring and thanking God is so fundamental to our design that
once men abandoned it, Paul tells us that they spiraled into futility and
darkness.

For although they knew God, they did not honor him as God or
give thanks to him, but they became futile in their thinking, and
their foolish hearts were darkened. Romans 1:21 ESV

Gratitude is so essential to our relationship with the Living God that
offerings of thanksgiving were part of the Law of Moses. Later on, King
David took additional steps to guard the importance of thanksgiving in
worship after he had returned the ark of the covenant to the Tabernacle:

Then he appointed some of the Levites as ministers before
the ark of the LORD, to invoke, to thank, and to praise
the LORD, the God of Israel. 1 Chronicles 16:4 ESV

Likewise, in the New Testament we see that "acceptable worship"
comes from a foundation of thankfulness for the new life God has
granted us:

Therefore let us be grateful for receiving a kingdom that cannot be shaken, and thus let us offer to God acceptable worship, with reverence and awe. Hebrews 12:28 ESV

And as we grow in Christ, thanksgiving will become second nature:

Let your roots grow down into him, and let your lives be built on him. Then your faith will grow strong in the truth you were taught, and you will overflow with thankfulness. Colossians 2:7 NLT

Giving thanks has always characterized those who sincerely love and serve the Lord: despite a royal decree against it, Daniel "prayed three times a day, just as he had always done, giving thanks to his God" (Daniel 6:10 NLT); along with every psalmist, Deborah, Hannah, Moses, Ezra, and others burst forth in song to express praise and thanks to God for His lovingkindness; Paul opened virtually every letter he wrote with words of thanks to God for the people who would read it. Jesus, who was one with the Father, took the time to thank Him for providing bread to feed thousands as well as celebrate the last supper with His disciples. None of these people, including Jesus, had an easy life, but all were grateful to God for what He had done. We can take encouragement from these examples, making gratitude a common trait in our lives:

And give thanks for everything to God the Father in the name of our Lord Jesus Christ. Ephesians 5:20 NLT

▶ What am I truly thankful to God for in my life? Have I ever made a list so I could see all the things He has done on my behalf?

....

....

....

....

▶ How often do I express my gratitude to Jesus aloud in prayer and worship?

....

....

....

....

▶ Do I spend more time complaining about my circumstances or thanking God for His work in my life?

....

....

....

....

▶ How can I encourage others to live grateful lives before their Savior?

....

....

....

....

MORNING

Confess that you can often be selfish in your gratitude
to Him, and ask that He change your heart to one that
is consistently grateful and honoring to Him.

Something like this. . .

*Lord, I confess and ask Your forgiveness for the selfish
way I often neglect to give You the thanks You deserve for
everything. I confess I get so distracted with new fears and
anxieties or the instant gratification of the world, that I fail
to make You the focus of my praise. Father, change my heart
to one of constant thanksgiving and praise to You.*

....

....

....

....

....

....

....

....

....

....

AFTERNOON

Ask for God to reveal the areas in your life in which
you spend more time complaining than thanking Him.

Something like this. . .

*Father, I often fail to understand or see my own actions
for what they are—instead, accusing and blaming others,
neglecting to see my own egotistical and thankless behavior.
Forgive me, Lord! Open my eyes in all areas, and reveal
to me new opportunities for growth in Christ!*

EVENING

Thank the Father for working in your life and
changing your heart to one filled with gratitude.

Something like this. . .

*Father Almighty, thank You for all that You do in
my life! Thank You for the constant reminders of
the promises You've made and followed through on!
Thank You for crafting within me a heart of gratitude,
and thank You for Your love and mercy when I do
not express as much gratitude to You as I should.*

....

....

....

....

....

....

....

....

....

....

....

....

DAY 19
GOOD WORKS

> But someone may well say, "You have faith and I
> have works; show me your faith without the works,
> and I will show you my faith by my works."
> JAMES 2:18 NASB

The Law of Moses was God's gift to His people to teach them and eventually to lead them to faith in His Messiah (Galatians 3:23-25). It was designed to drive people to their knees and cry out for help, not give them an opportunity to pat themselves on the back for their "good works." Some people got it; many did not. By the time of the Reformation, the notion that man participated in his own salvation by adding good works to his faith was actually part of church doctrine. If written as an equation, the idea the Reformers fought to correct would look like this:

Faith + Good Works = Salvation

This belief still lingers today because there's a certain appeal to the concept. Why shouldn't we be doing something to earn our place with God? Why shouldn't we get a few points for our righteous deeds? Why wouldn't God open up heaven to those who do good? To the worldly mind that seems completely reasonable. It's just not biblical. Paul emphasized the grace of God as the source of our salvation—completely apart from anything we can do to cause it:

> God saved you by his grace when you believed. And you can't
> take credit for this; it is a gift from God. Salvation is not a
> reward for the good things we have done, so none
> of us can boast about it. Ephesians 2:8-9 NLT

Salvation cannot be obtained by our own efforts. Period. It's a gift, and it comes from God through our faith not through our good works. Faith and works are always in opposition to each other when it comes to gaining salvation. Jesus cleverly pointed this out to some sincere folks who wanted to know how to work their way to eternal life:

*They replied, "We want to perform
God's works, too. What should we do?"*

*Jesus told them, "This is the only work God wants from you:
Believe in the one he has sent." John 6:28-29 NLT*

If you want to work to please God, work at believing was Jesus' message. Spend all your energy on faith because "without faith it is impossible to please Him" (Hebrews 11:6 NASB).

Although faith and works are counter to each other as a means of salvation, they have a cooperative relationship when it comes to living under grace. John Calvin wrote in his Antidote to the Council of Trent, "It is therefore faith alone which justifies, and yet the faith which justifies is not alone. . . ." Calvin was echoing the same thought as James—your faith must show up in works or it doesn't qualify as a faith at all. Good works are a consequence of a saving faith by the design of God:

*For we are God's masterpiece. He has created us
anew in Christ Jesus, so we can do the good things
he planned for us long ago. Ephesians 2:10 NLT*

Good works are also part of our inheritance from the Lord. Before we were raised with Christ, our works were as dead as we were—now they are as alive as we are! Our good works now point everyone to the Source of our new life:

*Let your light shine before men in such a way that
they may see your good works, and glorify your
Father who is in heaven. Matthew 5:16 NASB*

To return to a mathematical representation, God's plan might look more like this:

Grace × Faith = Salvation + Good Works

There's a place for good works, but it's not as a means of bringing us to God, but rather bringing God to the world.

▶ Do I firmly grasp that salvation is a gift and cannot be earned in any way by my own good works?

....

....

....

....

....

▶ Does my faith express itself in good works? Would anyone recognize God from the good things I do? How do I make sure He receives the glory for my works?

....

....

....

....

....

....

▶ Do I think of good works as something God has prepared for me to do or something I come up with on my own?

....

....

....

....

....

....

MORNING

**Ask the Father to give you a heart of service
that is content in His calling for you.**

Something like this. . .

*Father, I ask that You would prepare my heart to humbly
accept the good works You have made ready for me, knowing
that it is only through Your grace that I am able to do them.
Grant me a heart of service, so that no matter what those
works are, I would be excited and willing to complete them.*

....
....
....
....
....
....
....
....
....
....
....
....
....

AFTERNOON

Pray for His help against vanity and ego in good works.

Something like this...

Lord, in Your wisdom, keep me from straying into self-righteousness and vanity when doing good works for You. Help me to understand that the works You have laid before me are not of my own making but out of the overflow of Your kindness. I ask that You would guide me away from the pits of egotistical reward, granting me a humble heart that is ready to serve for Your glory alone.

....

....

....

....

....

....

....

....

....

....

....

....

....

EVENING

Ask the Lord to help you increase in your faithfulness,
so that your good works would bring glory to Him.

Something like this. . .

*Father, thank You for all the opportunities that You've
given me to increase and grow in faithfulness, and I ask
that You would continue to reveal the ways in which I could
bring glory to You. Open my eyes and soften my heart to the
works You would have me do, so that I wouldn't miss a single
chance to honor You and further Your Kingdom.*

DAY 20
A FATHER'S PERSPECTIVE

All these are the twelve tribes of Israel, and this is what their
father said to them when he blessed them. He blessed them,
every one with the blessing appropriate to him.
GENESIS 49:28 NASB

In Genesis 49, Jacob (renamed Israel after wrestling with the angel of God) was about to die. He called his sons before him to pronounce one final blessing. And from the things he said to them, he was under no illusions what kind of men they were and what each needed for the "people of Israel" to continue and grow. Judah for example was told that he would take first place among his brothers, though he was not the oldest; that he would take preeminence, and that the Savior would come from his line:

> "The scepter will not depart from Judah, nor the
> ruler's staff from his descendants, until the coming
> of the one to whom it belongs." Genesis 49:10 NLT

Having the Messiah as a descendent was indeed a blessing. But Israel's pronouncements were not all what we might call "blessings." For Judah to become first, Rueben, the firstborn, had to be demoted:

> "Reuben, you are my firstborn, my strength, the child
> of my vigorous youth. You are first in rank and first
> in power. But you are as unruly as a flood, and you
> will be first no longer." Genesis 49:3-4 NLT

Not the final words Reuben probably wanted from his father. The others also got various kinds of blessings too. Some harsh and some wonderful, but all very personalized: one would be rich, one would become a servant, one would be attacked but overcome, one would become a judge of the Israelites, two would be scattered among them. According to the judgment of their father, each son heard what he needed.

God, our Good Father, knows each of us and what is suitable and appropriate for us. He's crafted each of us as individuals. While our walk of faith is based on the objective truths of the written Word, it's also a subjective journey when it comes to the details of how we are to serve Him. There are things specific to each of us, that only our Father knows how to use to help us become more like His Son. And like the sons of Israel, we may not always like what we hear. So, we have to ask ourselves this: are the only blessings we're willing to receive from our Father in heaven the positive ones? Is a blessing of troubles or hardship still from the Lord? God's definition of a blessing can be quite different from ours. He intends to give us specifically what we need to grow into the image of His Son.

> *And have you forgotten the encouraging words God spoke to you as his children? He said, "My child, don't make light of the LORD's discipline, and don't give up when he corrects you. For the LORD disciplines those he loves, and he punishes each one he accepts as his child." Hebrews 12:5-6 NLT*

As a Father, God is bound to do us good whether we like it or not! The good news in harsh blessings is that our Father considers each of us intimately and loves us completely:

> *For you formed my inward parts; you knitted me together in my mother's womb. Psalm 139:13 ESV*

Our heavenly Father is trustworthy and wise—all the "blessings" He gives, He also tailors to each of us, knowing how best to conform us to the image of His Son (Romans 8:29).

▶ Is there any area of my life that I don't see as a blessing but that could be from the hand of God?

....

....

....

....

....

....

▶ Have I sought favor from God but not been willing to take correction? Have I clung to any sin or bitterness or selfish idea while still asking for God to bless me?

....

....

....

....

....

▶ Do I really believe that God is personally and intimately crafting my experiences so that I become more like Jesus?

....

....

....

....

....

MORNING

Ask God for understanding and for
courage to trust His plan for your life.

Something like this. . .

*Father, I ask for Your guidance and wisdom through
those difficult areas of my life where it's hard for me to
see Your blessings. Grant me courage regardless of how
overwhelming or arduous the path seems. I ask for understanding when facing those challenging areas, so I can
see Your blessings and loving lessons within.*

....

....

....

....

....

....

....

....

....

....

....

AFTERNOON

Confess any sin or bitterness you are holding onto, that would keep you from a willingness to take God's correction.

Something like this. . .

Heavenly Father, I ask Your forgiveness for the pride I've been clinging to. Father, You know my heart, and I cannot hide from You the strongholds of selfishness I have allowed to reside there. Help me to take Your loving correction, and mold me into someone who appreciates Your loving blessings with understanding and a humble heart.

EVENING

Pray for an open heart during the hardest times and confess when you allow your heart to harden.

Something like this. . .

Father, I confess that sometimes in my anger and frustration with life's difficulties, I allow my heart to harden, taking the worldly path of irritation and accusation. Forgive my quick impatience! Please help me to keep my heart open during whatever trials I must endure, trusting You to see me through to the paths You have lovingly crafted for me.

....
....
....
....
....
....
....
....
....
....
....

DAY 21
GRACE

> But now as the prophets foretold and as the eternal God has
> commanded, this message is made known to all Gentiles
> everywhere, so that they too might believe and obey him. All glory
> to the only wise God, through Jesus Christ, forever. Amen.
>
> ROMANS 16:26–27 NLT

Too often grace is used not as the reason to live a holy life, but an excuse not to. Preaching or encouraging holiness through spiritual disciplines is met with objections that those things are somehow "legalistic" and that any effort on our part in some way negates the "gift" of grace. Nothing could be more contrary to a biblical understanding of the Gospel! Obedience to God's commandments doesn't earn us God's favor, it's the result of God's favor. Obedience is a blessing, allowing us to walk with God. It was His wise and loving plan for us all from the beginning.

Grace allows obedience. Without grace, we remain slaves to the flesh. In fact, it's grace that actually works as a teacher in the things God expects of us:

> *For the grace of God has appeared, bringing salvation*
> *to all men, instructing us to deny ungodliness and*
> *worldly desires and to live sensibly, righteously,*
> *and godly in the present age. Titus 2:11–12 NASB*

Denying ungodliness simply means saying no to the things of the flesh. Those things are always wrong, no matter the circumstance, culture, or disposition. The apostle Paul gave the Galatian church a convenient starter list of the most obvious ones:

> *Now the works of the flesh are evident: sexual immorality,*
> *impurity, sensuality, idolatry, sorcery, enmity, strife, jealousy,*
> *fits of anger, rivalries, dissensions, divisions, envy, drunkenness,*
> *orgies, and things like these. Galatians 5:19–21 ESV*

Paul added "and things like these" for a very important reason—this list isn't exhaustive. He was highlighting only the obvious things—they were responsible to identify anything that was contrary to godly living.

"Worldly desires" aren't listed as concisely in scripture but can be readily identified by the mature believer:

> *In the same way we also, when we were children,*
> *were enslaved to the elementary principles*
> *of the world. Galatians 4:3 ESV*

These basic ideas of the world (sometimes translated "elemental spirits") are those things that lure men into creating an identity apart from God: success, wealth, fame, influence, political power, sexual prowess, possessions, admiration, etc. Those are all highly valued worldly achievements. But here's where it gets a little tricky. A believer can enjoy all of these things but only within the context of God's calling. If you gain riches as part of His grace (like Abraham), there are scriptures instructing you how to handle it. If you are famous or influential or powerful or admired (like Joseph, Daniel, or King David), grace will teach you how to use those things as gifts. Are you married? Then you should be an expert on sex. . . with the wife God's grace has given you! (Read the Song of Solomon if you need help. . .)

The main point is that, by God's grace, we must constantly judge whether the things of the world have gotten too much of a hold on us. We need to rely on grace to teach us to be focused on the Kingdom of God above anything the world offers. We can't afford to be crowded out from the calling we've received:

> *"As for what was sown among thorns, this is the*
> *one who hears the word, but the cares of the world*
> *and the deceitfulness of riches choke the word,*
> *and it proves unfruitful." Matthew 13:22 ESV*

Striving with everything in us to obey the Law of Christ isn't legalism, it's part of our new nature. We were called to "believe and obey," and that's a privilege only grace can allow.

▶ What is the hardest thing in God's Word for me to obey? Have I allowed grace to teach me what to do in that area?

....

....

....

....

▶ How does the loving-kindness of my Father motivate me to pursue Him? What does that look like in my daily life?

....

....

....

....

▶ Do I take advantage of grace as a way to avoid changing?

....

....

....

....

▶ Have I slipped into any habit that could be considered legalistic? Am I trying to earn something from God instead of living to please Him as my Father?

....

....

....

....

MORNING

Ask God for His grace to teach you how to guard your heart in all areas of life.

Something like this. . .

Father, grant me the wisdom and understanding to be spiritually responsible in all areas of my life. Teach me to guard my heart against the corrupt ideas of success and identity that the world tries to reinforce. In obedience to You, Lord, I find my real self.

....

....

....

....

....

....

....

....

....

....

....

AFTERNOON

Ask the Lord to let His work in you be a light to others.

Something like this. . .

*I pray for an obedient and patient heart, Lord,
and that You would change me into a man who is
holy and honoring and pleasing to You. Allow the
brokenness of my life and the healing of Your grace to
become an example of Your faithfulness to others. Amen.*

....

....

....

....

....

....

....

....

....

....

....

....

....

EVENING

**Ask the Lord for strength to be obedient
in the areas that are difficult for you.**

Something like this. . .

*Father I admit that there are areas in my life that I have
been pridefully clinging to, and I've been resisting Your voice.
I've taken advantage of grace and used it as an excuse to
continue in these worldly habits. Father, forgive me! I submit
absolutely to Your will! Instill within me a willing heart,
so that I may truly obey Your commands.*

DAY 22
THE FAITH JOURNEY

"Listen to me, you who pursue righteousness, you who seek
the LORD: . . . Look to Abraham your father and to Sarah
who bore you; for he was but one when I called him,
that I might bless him and multiply him."
ISAIAH 51:1-2 ESV

During one of the Israel's darkest hours—the Babylonian exile—God speaks comfort to His people by reminding them that they are a community founded on faith. The faith of Abraham and Sarah literally birthed a nation, and their descendants should be encouraged when looking back on their story. Today, we who follow Jesus are part of that family of faith launched by Abraham:

And if you are Christ's, then you are Abraham's offspring,
heirs according to promise. Galatians 3:29 ESV

Abraham's faith journey began when he was still called "Abram," living among his family and his people in Haran. God commanded him to leave all that he knew behind with only the promise of a new home:

Now the LORD said to Abram, "Go from your country
and your kindred and your father's house to the
land that I will show you." Genesis 12:1 ESV

Abraham's journey began with a choice: stay with the familiar, or trust in the promise of God for a new life and a new way of life. We start the same way. We get to watch the promise of our new life in Christ unfold over time. God didn't spell out all the details of the journey before it began for Abraham, and He doesn't for us either. Perhaps knowing of the hardships, battles and suffering ahead would have been too much for Abraham, derailing the journey before it began. Or maybe God didn't map out the whole journey in advance because living by faith means trusting in the One who calls us to walk the journey with Him.

God actually offered something more motivating than details. He offered hope for the future. God promised Abraham that he would become a great nation, that he would be blessed and honored, and that all the families of the earth would be blessed through him (Genesis

12:2–3). The scale of those promises must have been overwhelming to Abraham! But they pale in comparison to the blessings we are granted in Christ:

> *"No eye has seen, no ear has heard, and no*
> *mind has imagined what God has prepared*
> *for those who love him." 1 Corinthians 2:9 NLT*

What awaits the redeemed of Christ cannot adequately be put into words because it cannot be grasped fully by any human imagination.

Eventually, along Abraham's journey, God does get more specific, showing him the entire land of Canaan with the promise, "I am giving all this land, as far as you can see, to you and your descendants as a permanent possession" (Genesis 13:15 NLT). Abraham had walked with God faithfully, and God was able to share more about His plan. As we walk with the Lord, He will reveal more as we obey Him and learn to listen to the Spirit. He may speak to us either by strong inner guidance or by more direct means, as He did in Acts 9 with a man named Ananias. (He was given a vision to go to the home of a man named Judas on Straight Street, to pray for Saul of Tarsus to receive back his sight. That's pretty specific!) However God chooses to make Himself known to you, you will know it if you're walking in faith.

Abraham had many more faith experiences that can instruct us: allowing his nephew Lot to choose the best lands for himself because he valued family over property (Genesis 13:8); honoring the righteous king-priest, Melchizedek, with a tenth of his spoils (Genesis 14:20); declining the reward of the godless king of Sodom so that he would not have his name and reputation connected to them (Genesis 14:21–24); receiving the covenant with God by faith, offering Isaac as a sacrifice, and finding a wife for Isaac.

Like Abraham, our journey of faith will cover a lot of twists and turns. But it begins with knowing who calls us, trusting the One who promises us a future, and honoring Him as we walk together, remembering that Jesus is the Rock from which we were all formed.

▶ In what ways am I living a life of faith? Have I been growing in my faith this year?

....

....

....

....

▶ Are there any areas that I've been reluctant to turn over to God completely? Any area that I've tried to do things my own way?

....

....

....

....

▶ When was the last time I really felt that the Holy Spirit spoke to me? What was His guidance and how did I respond?

....

....

....

....

▶ Is there anyone in my life whom I can encourage to live by faith and who encourages me?

....

....

....

....

MORNING

**Ask for the Lord's guidance to propel
you forward in your faith journey.**

Something like this. . .

*Father, guide me into opportunities where I can grow in my
faith the most. I pray against the temptation of thinking I
do not need constant stretching! Direct me, Father, away
from the path of stagnation and complacency, so that I may
become a more faithful servant of Your Kingdom.*

AFTERNOON

Ask the Lord to guide you in developing encouraging
and fruitful relationships with those around you.

Something like this. . .

Lord, help me to see the ways in which I may be an
encouragement to the fellow believers around me, and
also open my heart to their encouragement as well,
so that together as Your people, we would grow
in our faith and trust in Your plan for us.

....

....

....

....

....

....

....

....

....

....

....

EVENING

Let go of the areas you have been reluctant to turn over to God, and ask for His comfort and guidance.

Something like this. . .

Lord God, I submit to You! I lay everything before You and ask that You cleanse me of my vanity and selfish desires. I have learned—and am still learning—that I cannot do things my own way. I need You! I make the choice to relinquish everything to You, and I will faithfully trust in Your plan for my life.

DAY 23
COVETOUSNESS

"You shall not covet your neighbor's wife, and you shall not desire your neighbor's house, his field or his male servant or his female servant, his ox or his donkey or anything that belongs to your neighbor."

DEUTERONOMY 5:21 NASB

The Ten Commandments were given to the people of Israel after they left Egypt as the foundation of their new relationship with the Almighty. These ten were unique, written on stone tablets by God Himself and stored in the ark of the covenant (Deuteronomy 10:4). And of those ten things, one is unique among them: covetousness.

What makes the tenth commandment different? It's entirely an inner quality, and often hard to quantify. The first nine commandments can be checked off the list, so to speak: No other gods or idols? Check. Honoring Mom and Dad? Yep. Cheating on my wife, murdering my neighbor, stealing from work? Nope, not this week. Envied someone's awesome career, sexy wife, house on the lake, status in the community? Let me get back to you on that. . .

The Hebrew word translated "covet" in Deuteronomy 5:21 ('avah) means "to desire, incline, wait longingly, wish, sigh, want, prefer." It's pretty clear when you break one of the other nine commandments, but coveting is largely undetectable, unless it's manifested in our words and actions. We might not even realize we're doing it ourselves at first. But God knew that coveting what others have would destroy not only the individual but the community He was building.

We need to be on our guard against ignoring or justifying covetousness in our own hearts. There are at least three things that grow from the soil of covetousness that we can watch for:

Discontentment. When we long for what others have, we are essentially complaining that God hasn't been as good to us as He has to them. Becoming discontent and jealous is the opposite of trusting Him:

For jealousy and selfishness are not God's kind of wisdom. Such things are earthly, unspiritual, and demonic. James 3:15 NLT

Conflict. Harboring envy in our hearts can't be contained forever and can only erupt at some point:

> *Let us not become boastful, challenging one another,*
> *envying one another. Galatians 5:26 NASB*

Idolatry. Ultimately, covetous habits become a form of worship. Things, people, opportunities, circumstances all get put on a pedestal and then command our actions. People enslaved by covetousness are serving false gods:

> *For you may be sure of this, that everyone who*
> *is sexually immoral or impure, or who is covetous*
> *(that is, an idolater), has no inheritance in the*
> *kingdom of Christ and God. Ephesians 5:5 ESV*

Like the Israelites of old, there's no place in church today for covetousness. We are called to live and serve one another graciously, in the power of the Holy Spirit, not allowing envy and jealously to destroy us individually or as a family of faith.

▶ Is there any area of my life where discontentment has made me vulnerable to the temptation to covet what others have?

....

....

....

....

....

▶ Am I grateful to God for the wife I have? Am I trusting God for a wife? Am I grateful to God for being single? Married, engaged, dating, or single—is there any woman I have feelings for whom I should not?

....

....

....

....

....

....

▶ Is there anyone whose career or financial situation annoys me, makes me feel inferior, or makes me envious?

....

....

....

....

....

MORNING

Confess your covetousness and pray that God will help you in the battle against discontentment.

Something like this. . .

Father, I confess that covetousness has become so ingrained within me that I often don't even notice it fosters resentment and stokes conflict. Please wash me of discontentment and selfish ways. Please help me to stand up and fight back, growing in the peace that comes from trusting in You.

....

....

....

....

....

....

....

....

....

....

....

....

AFTERNOON

**Ask the Father to help you let go of
discontentment in your work or career.**

Something like this. . .

*Lord, forgive me for the complaining and grumbling I've
done about my work. Instead of taking joy in what You've
provided, I've wasted time looking at others' success with
envy. My fear and covetousness have caused me to be
ungrateful, ignoring all that You've done for me. Heal my heart
and help focus my desires on honoring and trusting You.*

....
....
....
....
....
....
....
....
....
....
....
....

EVENING

Ask for a heart of gratefulness and contentedness in your relationships, whether married, dating, or single.

Something like this. . .

Father I ask that You help calm and strengthen my mind when the lies of covetousness attack me. Guard my heart from narcissistic and worldly thinking so that I may represent Christ in all my relationships. Show me how to serve those closest to me without comparing the relationships others have. I thank You for the state of life I'm in, because You have called me to it.

....

....

....

....

....

....

....

....

....

....

DAY 24
HEARING GOD

I will instruct you and teach you in the way you should go;
I will counsel you with my eye upon you. Be not like a horse
or a mule, without understanding, which must be curbed
with bit and bridle, or it will not stay near you.
PSALM 32:8-9 ESV

From the first chapter of Genesis when God spoke the heavens and the earth into existence and then clearly explained His expectations to humankind, God has been expressing Himself, directly and indirectly, to all men everywhere. Creation itself was crafted to be His first spokesman:

The heavens proclaim the glory of God. The skies display his craftsmanship. Day after day they continue to speak; night after night they make him known. They speak without a sound or word; their voice is never heard. Psalm 19:1-3 NLT

Whether men choose to listen to creation's message or not, God has designed the natural world to make Him known, day after day, night after night. This is why God can hold humankind responsible to acknowledge that He exists as both eternal and divine:

For ever since the world was created, people have seen the earth and sky. Through everything God made, they can clearly see his invisible qualities—his eternal power and divine nature. So they have no excuse for not knowing God. Romans 1:20 NLT

Despite man's fall into sin, in His infinite mercy, God allows everyone to clearly see what is invisible and hear truth without the need for any language. But God didn't stop with the witness of creation. He sent generations of prophets to speak to His people. Some witnessed the fruits of their efforts in the people's response—repentance, obedience, faith— others were ignored, persecuted, or killed.

God reveals Himself because He wants a response, and many men have responded along the way. Men like Abraham, Moses, and David spent decades hearing and being guided by God in various ways from open dialogue with the Almighty to dreams and visions, hardships, and the rebuke of others.

The ultimate issue is not how God speaks to us but whether we are willing to listen no matter what avenue He selects. He wants us to learn to listen. He wants us to internalize His ways of thinking and living. He wants us to become mature sons, walking with Him of our own accord, not constantly waiting to be pulled along like an animal.

The warning in today's verse is to avoid being "without understanding"—neither pulling back nor standing still, but moving along "in the way you should go." We are in an ongoing relationship with our Father, and He wants to communicate over a lifetime. To that end He has given us His Holy Spirit:

> *"But the Helper, the Holy Spirit, whom the Father will send in my name, he will teach you all things and bring to your remembrance all that I have said to you." John 14:26 ESV*

> *But when He, the Spirit of truth, comes, He will guide you into all the truth; for He will not speak on His own initiative, but whatever He hears, He will speak; and He will disclose to you what is to come. John 16:13 NASB*

Therefore, since we have such great promises from our Father, let us practice listening; let us meditate on His counsel; let us be encouraged by His rebuke; and "let us also keep in step with the Spirit" (Galatians 5:25 ESV) every day He grants us.

▶ Do I have the assurance that God speaks to me? Do I believe He counsels me personally?

....

....

....

....

▶ Have I been reluctant to act on anything that I felt was from God because I didn't want to risk being disappointed? Have I been waiting for Him to pull me along?

....

....

....

....

▶ Is there anything that I know to be my Father's will but have not pursued wholeheartedly?

....

....

....

....

▶ In what ways have I responded to the Spirit that made my Father in heaven happy?

....

....

....

MORNING

Ask the Lord to open your eyes and ears to His counsel.

Something like this. . .

Lord, as I go about my day, open my eyes and ears to Your counsel. Keep me from being distracted or unresponsive to You in any way. Please help me learn to listen so that I don't stand idle in my ignorance but instead move closer to You.

AFTERNOON

Ask God to help You wholeheartedly
take the opportunities that He provides.

Something like this. . .

*Father, I have had to be dragged along in too many areas of
my life because of fear or a lazy, unwilling attitude. Forgive
me, Lord. I humbly ask that You build within me a grateful
heart that would joyfully and enthusiastically take every
chance and opportunity to follow You in everything.*

EVENING

Thank and praise the Lord for speaking in your life,
and ask for greater understanding.

Something like this. . .

*Father, thank You for speaking to me and revealing to
me the way forward! You are eternal in Your faithfulness,
and I thank You for the comfort You provide and the love
You give. Grant me more understanding, so that I may
better follow the plan You have for my life.*

DAY 25
TWO RELATIONSHIPS
ALL MEN NEED

You then, my child, be strengthened by the grace
that is in Christ Jesus, and what you have heard from
me in the presence of many witnesses entrust to
faithful men, who will be able to teach others also.
2 TIMOTHY 2:1–2 ESV

God designed fathers to be our first mentors in life. So naturally, it's the hope of every boy to have a good dad—patient, encouraging, loving, and full of wisdom. Sadly, that's not everyone's story. But no matter what our individual experience was, at some point, we all need to seek the input of older, godly men to keep growing spiritually. An older, more experienced believer brings a unique perspective and a voice of accountability, training, and encouragement to speak into our lives.

A mentor doesn't have to be a pastor, a Bible study leader, or even a close friend, although they may be those as well. A mentor is someone who knows the Word of God and has been through a few spiritual battles, a man who has modeled faith as a way of life over years, a man who knows you well or is willing to get to know you well. And above all a mentor is a man you're willing to be accountable to and submit to for training in godliness.

All men need that voice. And in case you're wondering, virtually no stage of life is too late for a mentor. Moses got help from an older man when he was over 80! Just after Moses led the people out of Egypt, his father-in-law, Jethro the priest of Midian, came to greet him. When Jethro saw that Moses was the only judge in Israel, he exclaimed, "This is not good!" (Exodus 18:17 NLT). He went on to outline a judicial system that delegated the work to others and left Moses free to lead the growing nation. Jethro had been leading for a long time, and Moses was new to the role, despite his age. And Moses happily submitted:

*Moses listened to his father-in-law's advice
and followed his suggestions. Exodus 18:24 NLT*

The second relationship that all men need is someone to mentor. This is the basis of discipleship— how one generation passes on the knowledge and practice of godly living. Moses poured his life into Joshua from his youth (Numbers 11:28), following God's command to encourage and strengthen him (Deuteronomy 3:28). Joshua became Israel's leader after Moses, bringing the people into the Promised Land. Elisha was trained as a prophet by Elijah and received a double of the spirit of prophecy that had rested on his mentor (2 Kings 2:9). Peter and Barnabas both influenced and guided Mark, resulting in the Gospel we have that bears his name.

Paul set the example for being a mentor throughout his ministry. He poured his life into Timothy, Titus, and many others whom he sometimes referred to as his children in the faith, as in today's verse. The pattern is clear: those walking by faith receive from those who are further along the journey and pour into those who are newer to it.

Not feeling up to the task? You're not alone. But if you're willing to care for someone younger in the faith, then you can start. You'll need to be grounded in your own walk and have some knowledge of scripture, but discipleship is less about theological training (though that is important) than it is about walking consistently in God's revealed will: How to work as unto the Lord, how to care for your wife and children, how to conduct yourself in the church and with your next-door neighbor—these are all things you can help a new believer learn as long as you're doing them yourself. You don't have to become someone's "next" father—just care for, pray for, and speak truth to a young man who wants it. Model for the next generation what was and is still being modeled for you.

▶ Is there anyone in my life whom I could talk to about guiding me and holding me accountable?

....

....

....

....

▶ Is there any reason I wouldn't be able to help a younger man to grow in his faith?

....

....

....

....

▶ Does my church have opportunities for me to serve in discipleship?

....

....

....

....

▶ How can I begin preparing spiritually to become a better mentor when the time comes?

....

....

....

....

MORNING

Ask the Lord to mold you into someone ready to mentor.

Something like this. . .

Father, craft me into a man who can mentor in a way that honors You. Continue to work in my life to create within me a heart of service and humble wisdom, so that I may be of use to younger believers in need. Help me to lead by example according to the scriptures, so that my words of encouragement aren't hollow or hypocritical but instead built upon Your Word.

AFTERNOON

Ask the Father for the vulnerability to accept any
mentors He provides to you, despite your age.

Something like this. . .

*Father God, I pray that You open my heart to accept the
mentors You make available to me. I ask that neither a
prideful mind-set nor the cynicism of age nor the fear of
vulnerability would hinder me from accepting a man to speak
into my life. Guard my heart against pride when my failings
are exposed in loving accountability, trusting instead that
You have provided a helper in my faith journey.*

....

....

....

....

....

....

....

....

....

....

....

EVENING

Ask the Lord to reveal ways to be encouraging to those you mentor and to those who mentor you.

Something like this. . .

Lord, whether mentoring or being mentored, grant me the wisdom that when being helped I am respectful and intently listening and that when serving I don't let ego or the vanity of my role cause me to misunderstand or frustrate the ones I mentor. Please continue to increase my understanding of the responsibilities I have in both positions Lord, so that all of my relationships would be honoring to You.

DAY 26
THE BIG IDEA BEHIND SMALL THINGS

"He who is faithful in a very little thing is faithful
also in much; and he who is unrighteous in a
very little thing is unrighteous also in much."
LUKE 16:10 NASB

The world's idea of being faithful is basically, don't sweat the small stuff. If it's big enough, then it matters doing well. But that's about the most arbitrary standard possible—each one judging whether something is important enough to deserve his best efforts and attention. With this mindset, returning a borrowed hammer is different from returning a borrowed car. One really matters, while the other. . .not so much.

By contrast, Jesus says it's in the small things that true faithfulness is demonstrated. Why? Because it comes from the character of the one responsible for the task. Faithful people do things faithfully; they do not take responsibility lightly. They're faithful in little things, not because of the scale of the task but because of the nature of their own character; because of who they are, not what is asked.

Look at the perspective of a man who assigned tasks to his servants:

*"The master was full of praise. 'Well done, my good
and faithful servant. You have been faithful in handling
this small amount, so now I will give you many more
responsibilities. Let's celebrate together!' " Matthew 25:21 NLT*

The master could trust this man because he handled the "small amount" with integrity and skill. Who wouldn't value that when delegating responsibilities? And look at the reward the servant gets: more responsibility. Irresponsible people would call that a punishment!

Look at the example of Joseph after his brothers sold him into slavery. He ends up in the household of the captain of the guard, Potiphar. There, with God's blessing, his master notices Joseph's faithfulness and success in everything he was assigned. That leads to a big promotion:

So Potiphar gave Joseph complete administrative
responsibility over everything he owned. With
Joseph there, he didn't worry about a thing—
except what kind of food to eat! Genesis 39:6 NLT

For a busy official like Potiphar, Joseph is a dream come true. And Joseph embraces advancement and the additional responsibility. Later, when Potiphar hears his wife's accusation against Joseph, "his anger burned" (Genesis 39:19 NASB)—not at Joseph but at being forced to choose between his unfaithful Egyptian wife and a faithful Hebrew slave. As the late theologian Howard Hendricks pointed out, Potiphar would have had any other slave executed. Instead he puts Joseph into "the place where the king's prisoners were confined" (Genesis 39:20 NASB)—which was actually attached to Potiphar's own house! (Genesis 40:3 NASB). Again, Joseph's faithfulness and competence win him more responsibility:

The chief jailer committed to Joseph's charge all the
prisoners who were in the jail; so that whatever was
done there, he was responsible for it. Genesis 39:22 NASB

When the chief baker and chief cupbearer to Pharaoh wind up in the royal jail, Potiphar assigns Joseph to take care of their needs personally (Genesis 40:4). Why? Because even though Potiphar had treated Joseph unjustly, he knows Joseph's character.

Faithfulness is a character trait, a mind-set, and a habit. We have to develop it as the psalmist encourages us to do:

Trust in the LORD and do good; dwell in the land
and cultivate faithfulness. Psalm 37:3 NASB

If we grow in faithfulness we're growing in one of the fruits of the Spirit (Galatians 5:22) and showing the world who our Father is. If we walk faithfully in the "very little things" He promises much more for us.

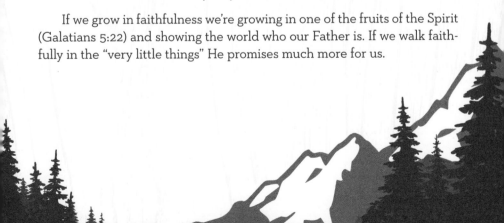

▶ In what areas of my life do I think I display faithfulness? What does it look like to others?

....

....

....

....

....

....

▶ Where is the Spirit offering me new opportunities of responsibility? How have I responded?

....

....

....

....

....

....

▶ What can I confess or change to become more faithful to God and to my commitments to others?

....

....

....

....

....

MORNING

Ask the Lord to show you opportunities to demonstrate faithfulness, no matter how small the task.

Something like this...

Almighty Father, as I go about my day, please reveal the ways I can demonstrate faithfulness to You by taking my responsibilities seriously. I ask that You fill me with the drive to complete my tasks to the absolute best of my ability no matter how trivial they may seem, and that in all diligence I honor You. Help me grow in character, so that I may earn even greater responsibility.

AFTERNOON

Confess the areas of your life where you have been
irresponsible, and ask Christ to change you.

Something like this. . .

*Lord, I confess that I have often been irresponsible
and flippant about things You've asked of me. Father,
I ask for Your forgiveness and that You would open my
eyes to see every task as a chance to practice faithfulness.
I reject the lies that say small-scale endeavors are worth less
effort or that having more responsibility is a punishment.
Father, please forge me into a man of character who
earnestly completes every task from You.*

....

....

....

....

....

....

....

....

....

....

EVENING

Ask the Lord to help increase your faithfulness,
despite unfair or difficult circumstances.

Something like this. . .

*Father, I ask that You guide and strengthen me during
unfair and difficult times so that my character remains
faithful and unwavering, rooted firmly in You. Though I
may suffer through injustice or opposition, I ask that You
help me in continuing to be responsible and giving every
effort to what You've laid before me, so that I may cultivate
faithfulness and increasingly honor You, Lord. Amen.*

DAY 27
SPIRITUAL WARFARE, PART 1

For we do not wrestle against flesh and blood, but against
the rulers, against the authorities, against the cosmic
powers over this present darkness, against the
spiritual forces of evil in the heavenly places.
EPHESIANS 6:12 ESV

"Spiritual warfare" can mean someone is suffering a terrible personal struggle, or it can describe an ungodly political proposal. One thing that seems to characterize it pretty consistently, however, is the idea of being under attack by the devil or his forces. But that's not quite the perspective of the scriptures. The truth is, in real spiritual warfare, we are being counterattacked. The enemy does not wage this war, he defends his position. It was Jesus Christ who started it:

*But the Son of God came to destroy
the works of the devil. 1 John 3:8 NLT*

The devil is trying desperately to keep his influence in this world, to keep his "kingdom" intact. When we follow Christ, we are pushing him back; we knock at his gates, not the other way around. The first recruits to this war received these compelling orders from their Commanding Officer:

*Behold, I have given you authority to tread on serpents
and scorpions, and over all the power of the enemy,
and nothing shall hurt you. Luke 10:19 ESV*

The disciples took the fight straight into enemy territory and came back rejoicing, saying, "Lord, even the demons are subject to us in your name!" (Luke 10:17 ESV). They had the enemy on the run because they fought for the rightful King. Later on, Paul got a similar assignment:

*". . .to open their [Gentiles] eyes so that they may
turn from darkness to light and from the dominion
of Satan to God, that they may receive forgiveness
of sins and an inheritance among those who have
been sanctified by faith in Me." Acts 26:18–19 NASB*

Paul and his companions literally carried the fight into the darkest parts of the known world, waging what he called "the good warfare" (1 Timothy 1:18 ESV). Not that the enemy took this lying down!

For we wanted to come to you—I, Paul, more than once—
and yet Satan hindered us. 1 Thessalonians 2:18 NASB

Like the angel who was hindered by spiritual forces for twenty-one days while Daniel prayed (Daniel 10), Paul faced serious opposition. The adversary is not going to stand idle while we expand God's Kingdom at his expense. He indeed counterattacks us to stop us, or at least slow our progress. If you're walking with Christ into battle, you will get the enemy's attention. Armies don't waste bullets on bystanders. But that's good news! You're doing what God planned for you!

While Satan has his tactics, we have ours. We are to put on the protection of God's armor to defend against the enemy's assaults, but critically important is the use of our God-given weapons:

Take the sword of the Spirit, which is
the word of God. Ephesians 6:17 NLT

Standing around in armor isn't the point. We are to use the weapons we're given to defeat the enemy. Prayer and the Word of God are our weapons. In the face-to-face battle between Jesus and the devil in the wilderness, Jesus Himself fasted and prayed, then quoted scripture in response to everything Satan threw at Him. In addition to those weapons, we've been given one vitally important thing: the promise of victory.

The God of peace will soon crush Satan under your feet. The
grace of our Lord Jesus be with you. Romans 16:20 NASB

Make no mistake, the conflict we're in requires faith and courage, and it requires preparation and training; sometimes we take ground quickly, and sometimes we need endurance. We may even lose ground sometimes. But we aren't the ones who should be afraid. We are marching with the King to a glorious future. He is the source of our strength.

▶ Is there an area in my life that I would say is under spiritual attack?

....

....

....

....

▶ What am I doing to advance the Kingdom that might be getting noticed by the enemy?

....

....

....

....

▶ How well am I prepared to wage a spiritual battle? Do I really understand how to use the right weapons?

....

....

....

....

▶ How can I get more training in spiritual combat?

....

....

....

....

....

MORNING

Ask the Lord to help you see your role
clearly in furthering His Kingdom.

Something like this. . .

*Eternal Father, prepare me for war! I confess and surrender
to You the areas in my life that I have allowed the enemy
to gain strongholds in, Lord. I ask that You wipe them out.
Train my hands for battle, and give me the confidence
that comes from following a righteous King.*

AFTERNOON

Ask the Father for comfort and healing when you feel as though you are exhausted and have lost ground.

Something like this. . .

My Savior, I need Your comfort—it's hard for me to see a clear path to victory because of the attacks I have endured. But I will hold fast, trusting in Your promises. Father, strengthen and embolden me to take back the ground I have lost. You are with me always, and I will continue to abide in You, knowing that my strength comes from You.

....

....

....

....

....

....

....

....

....

....

EVENING

Ask God for understanding about how
best to arm yourself for spiritual war.

Something like this. . .

*Father in heaven, give me wisdom and understanding to
fully clothe myself in the armor You supply; teach me how to
wield the sword of the Spirit. Give me opportunities for more
training to prepare for the spiritual battles to come. Help me
to be diligent and fruitful in all the preparation You provide,
so that I am ready to walk with Christ into battle.*

....

....

....

....

....

....

....

....

....

....

DAY 28
SPIRITUAL WARFARE, PART 2

So that Satan will not outsmart us.
For we are familiar with his evil schemes.
2 Corinthians 2:11 NLT

The devil fights dirty—no great surprise there! He will fight back as a cornered beast when confronted, but there's another kind of spiritual warfare he's more adept at: traps, snares, and enticements. These aren't about spears and arrows, but rather hooks, nets, and pits; strategy, planning, and patience; knowing our weaknesses and using them against us.

The goal of the enemy is entrapment, entanglement, and subjection. He wants us out of commission and unable to push into his territory. Traps can be more effective at neutralizing an opponent than winning a face-to-face battle. This has been Satan's strategy from the beginning:

"You won't die!" the serpent replied to the woman.
"God knows that your eyes will be opened as soon
as you eat it, and you will be like God, knowing
both good and evil." Genesis 3:4-5 NLT

Satan made it appear he was on our side, accusing God of withholding something special. And his plan worked pretty effectively. Humankind handed dominion of the world over to him. Deceit was the first tool of the enemy and continues to be his weapon of choice—to this day "Satan disguises himself as an angel of light" (2 Corinthians 11:14 NASB). Being taken out of the battle by the enemy through deception was a very real concern for the apostle Paul, as it should be for us:

But I am afraid that as the serpent deceived Eve by his
cunning, your thoughts will be led astray from a sincere
and pure devotion to Christ. 2 Corinthians 11:3 ESV

We are not immune to the enemy's traps because we believe in Christ. Recognizing traps before we fall into them is critically important. A famous example of this is the story of the Trojan Horse. Unable to overcome Troy's defenses by open conflict, the Greeks created a giant wooden horse as an apparent peace offering. Once the overconfident Trojans welcomed it into the city, out came the Greek soldiers hidden inside to open the gates for the rest of their army. It wasn't for lack of courage the Trojans were defeated—traps don't take courage and faith to face like a straightforward battle. Enticements and snares require wisdom and training to avoid.

How do we recognize something that is intentionally hidden? By growing in Christ, feeding on His Word as adults rather than spiritual infants. The mature practice their faith daily, under all kinds of conditions:

> But solid food is for the mature, who because
> of practice have their senses trained to discern
> good and evil. Hebrews 5:14 NASB

When you practice godly living, your spiritual perception grows. You will be able to see past appearances to the spiritual reality. Just after confessing Jesus as the Son of God, Peter pulled the Lord aside to rebuke Him for speaking about His upcoming suffering and death—Jesus saw something far different than a devoted follower:

> "Get behind Me, Satan! You are a stumbling block
> to Me; for you are not setting your mind on
> God's interests, but man's." Matthew 16:23 NASB

A mere human perspective might not have seen the trap that lay behind Peter's words, but Jesus clearly did.

Additionally, we need to keep alert, knowing we have an enemy who doesn't sleep. Mere common sense says we can't let our guard down around an enemy like that:

> Be sober-minded; be watchful. Your adversary
> the devil prowls around like a roaring lion,
> seeking someone to devour. 1 Peter 5:8 ESV

A prowling lion is an opportunistic hunter. We have to be on guard against that kind of enemy constantly. He's hungry and ruthless. . . but he's also on the run! Let us be prepared for his counterattacks, and wise about his schemes and traps. Victory in Christ in guaranteed—let us make every effort to enjoy the final moment of it with Him when He returns.

▶ What kinds of traps does the enemy normally set for me? How do I recognize them?

....
....
....
....
....

▶ Where have I left myself vulnerable to schemes and enticements?

....
....
....
....

▶ Am I staying prepared and on guard for surprise attacks?

....
....
....
....

▶ What am I doing to train my discernment of good and evil? Do I know anyone who can help me grow in this area?

....
....
....
....

MORNING

Ask the Lord for discernment in
recognizing the traps of the enemy.

Something like this. . .

*Loving Father, as I go about my day, I ask for Your wisdom
to recognize the traps of the enemy. Help me gain discernment, Lord, from a solid foundation in Your Word, to avoid
the pits and snares that I know will be put in my path.*

AFTERNOON

**Ask the Lord to help you guard any areas
where you've left yourself vulnerable.**

Something like this. . .

*Almighty God, forgive me for the places in my life that I
have left open to attack. I surrender, confess, and submit
those areas to You. I ask humbly that You would help me
repair, fortify, and guard those positions. Help me walk
in the freedom, peace, and healing I have in You.*

EVENING

**Ask the Lord to come to your aid when
you are isolated and being tempted.**

Something like this. . .

*Father, please come to my aid—I need Your strength
and peace to flow over me. Please grant me the courage
to make it through these temptations, reminding me that
I am covered by the blood of Christ and the sacrifice
You made to free me. Father, You are faithful beyond
measure, and I place my trust fully in You.*

DAY 29
MONEY, PART 1

Make sure that your character is free from the love of
money, being content with what you have; for He Himself
has said, "I WILL NEVER DESERT YOU, NOR WILL I EVER FORSAKE
YOU," so that we confidently say, "THE LORD IS MY HELPER,
I WILL NOT BE AFRAID. WHAT WILL MAN DO TO ME?"
HEBREWS 13:5-6 NASB

Money is an ingenious invention. In fact, it may be the most useful system humankind has ever created. It allows a man to figuratively carry one thousand cows in his pocket and trade them for whatever he likes, whenever he chooses, with whomever he wants. Amazing! It's almost magical in its convenience and scope. It allows a man to build a house without ever lifting a hammer. It allows a man to influence people he's never met. Money empowers a man with all kinds of possibilities—both good and evil.

The temptation to love money comes from the belief that it can do things it can't. It can't give us a real future because it's fickle and unstable:

As for the rich in this present age, charge them
not to be haughty, nor to set their hopes on the
uncertainty of riches, but on God, who richly provides
us with everything to enjoy. 1 Timothy 6:17 ESV

God is our hope and our provision. The reason money can't truly satisfy us is because it's a system designed for this world only—and we were designed for eternity. Money is so limited, in fact, that the richest man in the world once said,

Those who love money will never have enough.
How meaningless to think that wealth brings
true happiness! Ecclesiastes 5:10 NLT

King Solomon said much about wealth, and all from experience. He knew wealthy people who had no rest and poor people who slept soundly.

He knew those content with little and those discontent with much. He knew the key was whether people "loved" money. Jesus, who had no such direct experiences with wealth, was somewhat blunter:

"No one can serve two masters, for either he will hate the one and love the other, or he will be devoted to the one and despise the other. You cannot serve God and money. Matthew 6:24 ESV

Paul added to these warnings a reminder specifically to believers when he said:

For the love of money is a root of all sorts of evil, and some by longing for it have wandered away from the faith and pierced themselves with many griefs. 1 Timothy 6:10 NASB

All the warnings are basically this: money can be far too expensive! You can't afford to love it! Longing for wealth could be robbing you blind! As the English philosopher Francis Bacon once said, "Money is a great servant but a bad master."

It's our heart that determines whether we use money well, as a steward who must give an account. The godly uses of wealth are as profound as they are (or should be) obvious: Taking care of our own needs so as not to burden others unnecessarily (1 Thessalonians 4:11-12), taking care of our family's needs (1 Timothy 5:8) and providing for their future needs (Proverbs 13:22), taking care of the needy within the church (James 2:16, Romans 15:26, 1 John 3:17), helping the poor outside the church (Galatians 2:10), spreading the Gospel (Philippians 4:16), supporting the church and those who minister to us (Galatians 6:6), and at every opportunity honoring God by showing hospitality and generosity (Proverbs 11:25, 1 Timothy 6:18).

We must always be on guard against the whisper that says money can do for us what it cannot. If money has captured our heart, we'll never be content and we'll miss out on what true riches are.

▶ If I'm being completely honest with myself, would I say that money has an unhealthy hold on my thinking?

....

....

....

....

....

▶ Do I spend my efforts pursuing wealth to the exclusion of spiritual things?

....

....

....

....

▶ How am I doing in the righteous use of what I have right now?

....

....

....

....

▶ What can I do to become a better steward of what God has given me?

....

....

....

....

MORNING

Ask your Father to aid you in the struggle against excessively desiring worldly and material comforts.

Something like this. . .

Lord God, I admit to You my struggles with desiring the comfort and safety of wealth. Take away from me that focus on material things instead of You! Father, help me to better understand the purpose of money so that I honor You in every way with it.

AFTERNOON

Ask the Lord to reveal opportunities to be a responsible steward of what He's given you.

Something like this. . .

Father God, open my eyes to those in need, and reveal the opportunities in which I can share what You've provided for me. I ask also that You soften my heart and keep me from ever looking down on those with less, understanding that I am receiving everything from You and not by the work of my own hands.

....

....

....

....

....

....

....

....

....

....

....

....

EVENING

Ask God to shape your mind so that your efforts are refocused onto His plan.

Something like this. . .

Heavenly Father, I admit that I have wasted too much effort chasing wealth and comfort and have often neglected walking the path You've set before me. Please forgive me, Lord, and guide my efforts to be honoring to You. Continue working in me every day to focus on wholeheartedly living for Christ.

....

....

....

....

....

....

....

....

....

....

....

....

DAY 30
MONEY, PART 2

"Do not worry then, saying, 'What will we eat?' or 'What will we drink?' or 'What will we wear for clothing?' For the Gentiles eagerly seek all these things; for your heavenly Father knows that you need all these things. But seek first His kingdom and His righteousness, and all these things will be added to you."
MATTHEW 6:31-33 NASB

The desire for excess (the "love of money") is not the only way we can become preoccupied with finances. On the opposite end of the spectrum is the fear of want or poverty. The lure of wealth and the lack of it are both temptations to forget the proper place for, and use of, money.

Jesus' admonition to "seek first His kingdom and His righteousness" is about prioritizing our passions. If we obsess over our own needs (even legitimate ones), we'll never get beyond them. We'll fill our days with anxiety rather than the things of God.

Our needs are well known to our caring Father. His primary means of providing for the needs of His people has always been honest work. Moses, speaking to the Israelites—newly released from slavery—reminded them that anything they earned for themselves as free men was still a gift from above:

You shall remember the LORD your God, for it is he who gives you power to get wealth, that he may confirm his covenant that he swore to your fathers, as it is this day. Deuteronomy 8:18 ESV

But we all have different stories of how our Father apportions that "power to get wealth." One size doesn't fit all. Most of us have probably experienced a range of financial circumstances throughout our lives. The apostle Paul knew what that felt like. His income often went in cycles, sometimes earning his own way making tents, sometimes being supported by churches. But from his experiences with money, he grew in his faith:

I know how to live on almost nothing or with everything. I have learned the secret of living in every situation,

*whether it is with a full stomach or empty, with plenty
or little. For I can do everything through Christ,
who gives me strength. Philippians 4:12-13 NLT*

His "secret" is one of the most quoted verses in the Bible. Unfortunately, most people miss an important point—Paul "learned" the secret, like you might learn to play golf. He did it over time and from lots of direct experience. He didn't discover some hidden secret, so much as learn a life lesson; no sudden revelation but an ongoing challenge to trust God.

No one, even an apostle, has a guaranteed income. What we have is the promise of God to care for us. But you can't blame God if our need arises from being lazy or foolish with money:

*The foolishness of man ruins his way, and his
heart rages against the LORD. Proverbs 19:3 NASB*

We are to be stewards of what He provides, however He provides it. It's all His to begin with. That's why, even in humble circumstances we are to be generous. Paul commended the example of the Macedonian church in this regard:

*For they gave according to their means, as I can testify, and beyond
their means, of their own accord, begging us earnestly for the favor
of taking part in the relief of the saints. 2 Corinthians 8:3-4 ESV*

Paul goes on to tell the Corinthians:

*The point is this: whoever sows sparingly will also reap
sparingly, and whoever sows bountifully will also reap
bountifully. Each one must give as he has decided in his heart,
not reluctantly or under compulsion, for God loves a cheerful
giver. And God is able to make all grace abound to you,
so that having all sufficiency in all things at all times, you
may abound in every good work. 2 Corinthians 9:6-8 ESV*

We either understand where money comes from or we don't. We either follow His example of generosity, or we stay on the hamster wheel with the "Gentiles" eagerly and anxiously seeking to fill needs that will never end.

▶ Do I really believe that God will take care of my needs as I put Him first?

....

....

....

....

▶ How much do I worry over finances? Does it occupy my thinking to distraction?

....

....

....

....

▶ What specific issues am I most concerned about in my finances? Is there anyone who can help me seek God on these issues?

....

....

....

....

▶ Is there anything I need to confess or repent of concerning fear, anxiety, or preoccupation with money?

....

....

....

....

MORNING

Confess your fear and anxiety over finances
and ask that the Lord would grant you peace.

Something like this. . .

*Almighty Father, I confess and lay my fears and anxiety
about my finances before You—forgive me for not fully
placing my trust in You. Give me the strength and courage
to face and overcome these fears, wholeheartedly placing
my faith in Your promises to take care of me.*

....

....

....

....

....

....

....

....

....

....

....

....

AFTERNOON

Ask the Lord to help keep you from
being mentally consumed with money.

Something like this. . .

*Father God, I ask that You guide my mind away from being
consumed with the distraction of money. I have spent so long
dwelling on these things that it affects my day-to-day ability
to focus on what You would have me do. I have often made
money into an idol, and for that, Lord, I ask that You would
forgive me. Change my exhausted and fearful mind into one
that is renewed and focused completely on You.*

EVENING

Ask the Lord for a heart that is
content in what He has provided.

Something like this...

*Lord, I thank and praise You for everything You've given me!
Thank You for taking care of me even when I act selfish and
discontent. Help me to always accept Your provision with
joy. Please help me to take refuge and comfort in You alone,
remembering that real contentment comes from You.*

Thank You, Father! Amen.